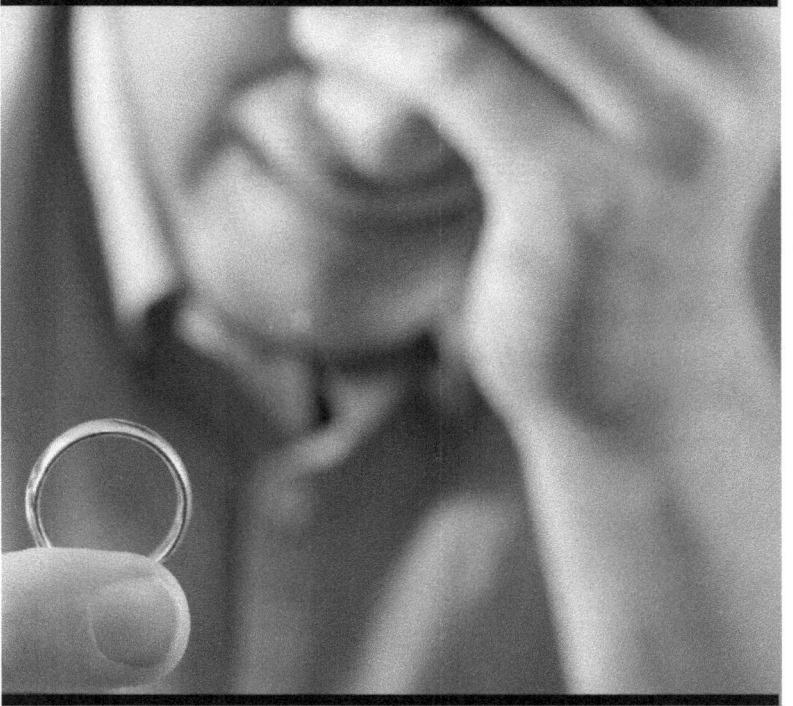

# DECEIVED

How Errors in a Faith System Affect Both God & His People.

JEANNE METCALF

*"Know therefore that YeHoVaH your God, he is God, the faithful God, which keeps covenant and mercy with them that love him and keep his commandments to a thousand generations ...*

*Deuteronomy 7:9*

International Copyright © 2025
Cegullah Publishing & Apologetics Academy
All rights reserved.

CP & AA

**Textbook: ISBN #: 978-1-998561-04-9**
**Workbook: ISBN # 978-1-998561-05-6**

Cover Design by: Jeanne Metcalf
Image: i-Stock 657028012

# *Please note:*

### "DECEIVED"

(How Errors in a Faith System
Affect Both God and Man)

**Textbook: ISBN #: 978-1-998561-04-9**
**Workbook: ISBN # 978-1-998561-05-6**

**This is Book 1 on the topic of deception.**

### "The Coming Deception"

(How to Recognize
the Man of Sin,
the Son of Perdition)

Textbook: ISBN #: 978-1-998561-06-3
Workbook: ISBN # 978-1-998561-07-0

**This is Book 2 on this topic of deception.**

You can read either book on its own, but to get the most out of this subject on deception, we suggest Book 1 be read first.

# COPYRIGHT MATTERS

This book is an original manuscript by the author, protected by international copyright laws of Canada. Therefore, none of this author's work may be reproduced, in part or in whole, or stored in a retrieval system, or transmitted in any form or by any means, electronic, mechanical, photocopied, recorded or otherwise for commercial use without the *prior written* permission of the author. However, it is possible to receive permission to use short quotations for personal use, or use in a group study, or for permission to copy certain passages, or to make portions of the writings available for overhead viewing. Simply, contact the author[1] or publisher to request it.

# SCRIPTURE MATTERS

*All scripture quotes **originate from** or **are formed around** the **KJV** of the Bible, **public domain**. In places, some alterations occur in the text changing ye, thee or thou or other KJV terms to modern English. Additionally, the name of God appears as YeHoVaH, rather than LORD and Yeshua rather than Jesus, to honour His Jewishness. See appendix for more information as to why we make these changes.*

---

[1] See Contact Page in Appendix

## DEDICATION

Deception brings with it darkness, disappointment and sorrow, but when the light of God breaks through, it ends the grief. With the latter end in mind, I dedicate this book to any person ever broken or touched by deception.

For such a precious one, I pray that the God of all comfort visits you. As He shines His light of truth into your life, may His restoration spring forth speedily.

*"Weeping may endure for a night, but joy comes in the morning."*

*Psalm 30:5*

# DECEIVED

## COURSE 601

### Section I: Deception Averted

|   |   |   |
|---|---|---|
|   | Introduction............................................ | 11 |
| 1. | A Chosen Covenant................................ | 21 |
| 2. | A Perfect Pattern.................................... | 33 |

### Section 2: Deception Patterns

| 3. | A Shrouded Scheme............................... | 51 |
|---|---|---|
| 4. | A Destined Disaster................................ | 65 |
| 5. | A Deceptive Devotion............................. | 79 |
| 6. | A Sinister Snare...................................... | 93 |

## COURSE 602

| 7. | A Corrupted Counsel.............................. | 109 |
|---|---|---|
| 8. | A Perilous Partnership........................... | 123 |
| 9. | A Deadly Defence................................... | 139 |
| 10. | A Passionate Pursuit.............................. | 153 |

### Section 3: Deception Conquered

| 11. | A Righteous Relationship...................... | 167 |
|---|---|---|
| 12. | A Corrected Course................................ | 185 |
|   | Conclusion............................................. | 203 |

# APPENDIX

| | |
|---|---|
| About King James Version............................. | 217 |
| About Jeanne Metcalf................................... | 232 |
| About CP & AA........................................... | 234 |
| A Name to Honour...................................... | 211 |
| Books by Jeanne Metcalf............................... | 229 |
| Contact CP & AA......................................... | 236 |
| Salvation Message....................................... | 218 |
| Scripture Index........................................... | 224 |
| Sinner's Prayer & Lifetime Commitment............ | 222 |

# COURSE 601

DECEIVED

Section 1: Deception Averted

כתונה

The above Hebrew word, taken from the picture in Section 1 says ketubah. A Ketubah is a marriage contract

## Introduction

*"Pilate said unto him, What is truth? And when he had said this, he went out again unto the Jews, and said unto them, I find in him no fault at all."*

John 18:38

**D**ECEIVED, A STATE OF BEING most people prefer to avoid, ignores all social protocol and comes a courting. Its root, deception, knocks with a gentle sound at a person's door, and innocently smiles at its intended victims. Bit by bit, one inch at a time, it draws its victims into its snare. Then, as its unsuspecting victims let down their guard and willingly receive it, deception enters to further spin its web of deceit.

Whether it is mental, emotional or spiritual invasion, deception cares not. It works to penetrate every area of its victims' life. Deception's major goal aims to control, manipulate and coerce its victims to keep them trapped within its grasp. Active, cruel, insanely possessive and deadly, are but a few words to describe deception and its behaviour towards its victims.

## DECEIVED.
### How Errors in a Faith System Affect Both God & His People

Most of us know deception exists but prefer we never encounter it. Unfortunately, knowing it exists only *partially* prepares us to avoid it. To overcome any form of deception, we need a proactive approach. That is true in every facet of the world around us, including the field of faith. In fact, Yeshua warned His disciples of deception:

> *Mark 13:22-23*
> *"For false Christs and false prophets shall rise, and shall show signs and wonders, to seduce, if it were possible, even the elect. But take heed: behold, I have foretold you all things."*

Yeshua's warning, *"take heed"*, indicated that Yeshua required His disciples to pay attention to the coming deception before His return. Therefore, believers must be alert for false Messiah's. In other words, people who present themselves as being the answer, or having all the answers. In their presentation, they become so convincing, that, if it were possible, they would *seduce* even the very elect.

Note the word "seduce". To seduce refers to the disarming of one's defences. It suggests an attempt to lower the protective wall of the very elect, *(believers in the kingdom of God)*. To put it another way, deception attempts to neutralise one's objections. It tricks people into accepting a new reality, one which seems good but hidden beneath the surface lay a devious and hidden agenda. Deception, like an adulterer, persuades another to unite with its agenda. With logic, or in some cases with lying signs and wonders, it strategizes to pull believers off course.

No believer can afford to disregard deception's existence nor its attempts to thwart their walk with God. Rather, wisdom teaches believers to be on guard to recognize deception's lies and likewise, to employ a defensive mindset to ensure freedom from deception's deadly snare.

## DECEPTION PREVENTION

Before discussing some practical examples, let us look at a simple analogy. Consider how banks train tellers to recognize counterfeit bills. Surprisingly enough, they do not bring the tellers counterfeit bills to study. These are too numerous to examine. Additionally, counterfeiters continue to invent new and improved methods to fool the unsuspecting eye. Therefore, the best line of defence in recognizing the counterfeit lies in knowing the original.

As bankers examine the original, they put their senses of sight and touch to work. With touch, they feel the texture of the printing on the bill. Counterfeits feel different than the original.

Next, using their eyes, they check for a watermark or other things on specific bills which only appear on  the original. Depending on the bill, they might tilt it to see if certain numbers or characters change in the light just as they were designed to do. On other bills they look for fine-line printing and tiny text to ensure they are neither blurred nor missing. While this task seems rather simple, this method produces enough evidence (**facts**) to detect counterfeit (**fake**) currency.

Using this same principle of knowing the original works well, too, in identifying other forms of deception. Afterall, counterfeits of original things appear everywhere and, on every front, challenging one to question the difference between the real and the fake. Even from ancient times, people, confused by counterfeit leaders, sought for the original, including in the time of Yeshua.

During the trial of Yeshua, for example, the Roman governor of Judea, Pontius Pilate, asked Yeshua this question:

**"What is truth?"**

Yeshua's earlier remarks to Pilate no doubt sparked that question when He said,

Introduction

*John 18:37*
*"Pilate therefore said unto him, Are you a king then? Jesus answered, you say that I am a king. To this end was I born, and for this cause came I into the world, that I should bear witness unto the truth. Every one that is of the truth hears my voice."*

Pilate, just like every other person, had his questions what does or does not constitute truth. Yet, in this historic scene familiar to Christians, we understand by God's divine Word that the true King of Israel stood before Pilate.

*John 1:49*
*"Nathanael answered and said unto him, Rabbi, you are the Son of God; you are the King of Israel."*

To take it one revelation further, Truth, Himself, stood before Pilate!

*John 14:6*
*"Jesus said unto him, I am the way, the truth, and the life: no man comes unto the Father, but by me."*

In the case with Pilate, he saw, talked with, and judged Truth, but the man knew it not! Deception held him in its grip.

Today like Pilate, many people fail to recognize Yeshua as truth because deception acts just like it did in years gone by. It sets its sights on every person no matter their age or station in life. Deception tosses its invisible veil of unbelief on all unsuspecting people. Indeed, deception reaches out its grip on every front, especially targeting the ones hungering for truth. Fortunately, scripture provides us with the answer to finding truth:

*Jeremiah 29:13*
   *"And you shall seek me, and find me, when you shall search for me with all your heart."*

Here, then, stands the promise of God for all who pursue Him. Here lies the reality of discovering truth and walking in it!

**One must seek God (Who is Truth) with all their heart.**

In other words, if we want to know God and walk in a life of truth, its door stands ready to open to all who seek God *with every aspect of their being.* In doing so, our searching for truth ends with a true, fruit bearing encounter with God.

## However, we cannot stop there!

Our walk with God brings forth deep truth in every area of our life, and thus our pursuit of truth never ends. Rather, as we walk through the open door to truth, we enjoin ourselves to truth and thus walk through this life, hand in hand with Him. Nevertheless, we must still be on guard for deception, especially as we near the time of Messiah's return.

Therefore, let us link arm in arm with the solution to deception. Let us persist in seeking God with all our heart, mind, soul and strength, vigorously preparing for coming deception's traps that might arise. Let us learn well the facts that scripture presents and in doing so, become fortified against anything false (fake).

Additionally, as each believer shares those solid scriptural concepts (facts) with others, it presents a broader field of defence for all who care to listen. To truly understand the truth, therefore, let us take a lesson from the bank teller's training. In doing so, let us investigate and study aspects of the original from all sides. In that way we fortify ourselves.

## ANOTHER ANALOGY

Throughout the first and second covenants, scripture presents an analogy of God, the Father, as well as Yeshua, the Son, as the bridegroom and the body of believers as the bride. In both covenants, scripture addresses the bride's unfaithfulness to her husband.

Under the first covenant, we hear of times when Israel's unfaithfulness to covenant grieved the husband's heart[2]. Unfortunately, it was not a onetime occurrence, either. Eventually, due to a constant, continual betrayal, the Bible speaks of God's intentions to divorce Israel for her adultery[3]. Fortunately, with God's mercy in place, in a promised future time, Israel, repents and returns to God.

Within the second covenant, scriptures address the unfaithfulness of the bride to the groom, many of which we find in passages within the book of Revelation. In Yeshua's address to the seven churches, we hear about operative practices or teachings[4] which broke covenant with God and offended Him.

## GOAL OF THIS BOOK
Having discussed the reality of deception in this introduction, including Yeshua's warning of

---

[2] Hence the explanation of the cover photo showing a husband grieving over his wife who broke covenant with him.

[3] *Jeremiah 3:1 "They say, If a man put away his wife, and she go from him, and become another man's, shall he return unto her again? shall not that land be greatly polluted? but you have played the harlot with many lovers; yet return again to me, said YeHoVaH."*

[4] *Revelation 2:20 "Notwithstanding I have a few things against you, because you allow that woman Jezebel, which calleth herself a prophetess, to teach and to seduce my servants to commit fornication, and to eat things sacrificed unto idols."*

deception's increase in the times preceding His return, it becomes the objective of this book to bring to the front biblical warning regarding deception, its tactics and devices.

Surprisingly enough, as we study this topic together, we will see that deception emerges in various ways to deceive the unaware. It might wear a different face, dress itself in a changed garment, but it is the same deception. Or, at times, when deception becomes overconfident, it may well present itself in the same form as it did in the past, even using its former name[5]!

To discover deception's deceiving tactics, as we journey together through this book, we examine examples of deception revealed in scripture. Since deception causes great pain to those snared in its grasp, by looking at the many patterns of deception outlined in scripture, one develops a sharp discernment and thus obtains an edge on recognizing the counterfeit. As we see those examples or patterns of the counterfeit, we better tune our ears to receive scripture's warnings as these patterns convey facts very applicable to today.

---

[5] For example, the teachings of Baalim in *Revelation 2:14*. *"But I have a few things against you, because you have there them that hold the doctrine of Balaam, who taught Balac to cast a stumblingblock before the children of Israel, to eat things sacrificed unto idols, and to commit fornication."*

Within Section 1 entitled, *Deception Averted*, in chapters one and two, readers examine a positive pattern of God's presence in the midst of His people. This pattern serves as an example showing what God requires of believers, as well as what benefits them. In Section 2, we look at *Deception Patterns*. Here, readers explore situations that God recorded to give His people knowledge of the practises of deception. Finally, in Section 3, *Deception Defeated*, we can rejoice together as we see how God empowers believers to overcome deception.

Prepare yourself for a short journey into the scriptures to discover some positive realities about the God of the Bible, as well as many things that the Bible reveals regarding the deadly tactics of deception.

Dear reader, may YeHoVaH, the God of all heaven and earth, grant insight into His Word. May He open the depths of His heavenly wisdom to give you understanding and clarity as you peer into the topic of deception.

May we all embrace the lessons here, so none become

**DECEIVED.**

May each person discover the truth regarding

*How errors in a faith system affect both God and His people.*

# 1

## A Chosen Covenant

*"For you are a holy people unto YeHoVaH, your Elohim, YeHoVaH, your Elohim has chosen you to be a special people unto himself, above all people that are upon the face of the earth."*

*Deuteronomy 7:6*

**TO EXAMINE THE ORIGINAL** pattern showing God's presence in our midst, we begin by looking at the best example of this topic given in scripture. That example comes forward at the same time as the birth of the nation of Israel[6]. At that time as God chose Israel to be His special nation, He bound them to Him through a wedding like contract called a **ketubah.** This legal binding agreement, classified as a covenant, contained within it, promises unique to the individual partners of the marriage; things they promise to each other. It also included penalties which automatically came into effect if any party failed to meet the terms of the agreement.

---

[6] Jacob's descendants.

*Exodus 34:10*
"And he said, Behold, I make a covenant: before all your people I will do marvels, such as have not been done in all the earth, nor in any nation: and all the people among which you live shall see the work of YeHoVaH: for it [is] a terrible[7] thing that I will do with you."

Regarding the terms of that covenant between God and His people, scripture clearly outlined God's part and Israel's, too. This covenant solidified, first, the immediate generation of Israel, *(the fathers)*, of the covenant and then, included the generations to come. We see this as God specifically commanded Israel to teach their children the terms of the covenant, thus making it span from generation to generation.

*1 Chronicles 16:15-17*
"Be you mindful always of his covenant; the word [which] he commanded to a thousand generations; [Even of the covenant] which he made with Abraham, and of his oath unto Isaac; And has confirmed the same to Jacob for a law, [and] to Israel [for] an everlasting <5769>" covenant,

---

[7] Old English word meaning awesome.

## Chapter 1:
## A Chosen Covenant

In Hebrew, the word for everlasting[8] is עולם, (Olam). עולם (Olam) means continuous existence, perpetual, or for a very long time. Looking deeper into its meaning, it shows something hidden or concealed. Its literal translation means *beyond the horizon*[9], therefore, suggesting that as long as a horizon exists, the covenant continues.

Looking at the word עולם (Olam), then, we easily recognize that the timeframe of the covenant YeHoVaH made with Israel, He intended to span way past the first generation. In other words, עולם, (Olam) implies the length of time of the covenant agreement between YeHoVaH and His people goes beyond the horizon.

This timeframe we see reaffirmed in other scriptures such as in 1 Chronicles 16:15. It states: *to a thousand generations, which presents the same idea as the word Olam, implying a long time.* Then in 1 Chronicles 16:17 He uses the word עולם, (Olam) again, meaning, beyond the horizon, or until no more tomorrows come. All of this indicates a very long time.

---

[8] Strong's Concordance # 5769 does not include the vav as does the Ancient Hebrew Research Centre.
[9] Ancient Hebrew Research Centre https://www.ancient-hebrew.org/definition/eternity.htm

Regarding the other terms of the covenant, YeHoVaH clearly defined them. Those covenant terms YeHoVaH presented to His people through Moses as His mediator at the base of Mt. Sinai in Arabia, *after* YeHoVaH brought them out of Egypt.

Let us look at the terms of the ketubah (wedding covenant) which Moses mediated.

| HUSBAND: | YeHoVaH's VOWS |
|---|---|

*Exodus 19:5-6*
*"Now therefore, if you will obey my voice indeed, and keep my covenant, then you shall be a peculiar treasure <5459 סְגֻלָּה cëgullah > unto me above all people: for all the earth is my: And you shall be unto me a kingdom of priests, and a holy nation."*

Here, YeHoVaH calls the people His cegullah, a unique and endearing term. Cegullah means something rare, treasured, and out of the ordinary like a rare jewel. Like a solitaire in a ring, Israel stood out, apart from the other nations upon the earth. Calling Israel YeHoVaH's cegullah meant that, *in His eyes*, Israel as His wife, was a precious treasure, rare and unique. Furthermore, in using that word, cegullah, YeHoVaH promised to treasure Israel, drawing her close, as a husband draws his bride near to him. Moreover, YeHoVaH promised in this ketubah

## Chapter 1:
### A Chosen Covenant

(wedding contract), to keep Himself for His bride alone, and she *in turn* must keep herself for Him alone.

Moses acts as the mediator or the negotiator of this covenant. First, he speaks with YeHoVaH, (the groom). Then, having received the groom's requirements regarding the bride, Moses relates those exact terms to Israel, the bride, to get her response.

**BRIDE:** **ISRAEL'S VOWS**

*Exodus 19:7-8*
> "And Moses came and called for the elders of the people and laid before their faces all these words which YeHoVaH commanded him. And all the people answered together, and said, all that YeHoVaH has spoken we will do. And Moses returned the words of the people unto YeHoVaH."

Moses collects Israel's leaders together as these are the legal spokesmen for the nation. He relates YeHoVaH's requirements of the bride (Israel). Then, he receives their response to the proposal. Next, still acting as mediator, Moses returns to YeHoVaH with Israel's (the bride's) response, which was agreeable.

After YeHoVaH receives an affirmative response, He tells Moses to ready the people. He is going to come down and speak to them directly, but His coming requires certain preparations. Moses conveys the conditions and ensures the people get ready, prepared just as YeHoVaH required. Then, on the third day as promised, YeHoVaH appears in a thick cloud on the mountain top, accompanied by loud thunder cracks and lightning as well as blaring shofars (trumpets).

In this scene of YeHoVaH's powerful entrance, He speaks very specific covenant terms to Israel, what we later called the ten commandments. However, YeHoVaH's voice was so piercing that they thought they would all die. Terrified by His voice, the Israelites demanded YeHoVaH stop speaking directly to them.

*Exodus 20:18-19*
> *"And all the people saw the thunderings, and the lightnings, and the noise of the trumpet, and the mountain smoking: and when the people saw it, they removed and stood afar off. And they said unto Moses, speak you with us, and we will hear but let not God speak with us, lest we die."*

Fortunately, their initial rejection of this direct encounter with YeHoVaH did not deter the acceptance of the covenant. In His mercy, YeHoVaH provided a further opportunity for Israel to seal the covenant with Him.

YeHoVaH calls Moses and relates to him the covenant terms. Moses then writes them in a book and presents the book to the people. They listen to Moses reading it and then agree to those terms.

> *Exodus 24:3*
> "And Moses came and told the people all the words of YeHoVaH, and all the judgments: and all the people answered with one voice, and said, All the words which YeHoVaH has said will we do."

Next, a blood covenant solidified or sealed the contract.

> *Exodus 24:4-8*
> "And Moses wrote all the words of YeHoVaH, and rose up early in the morning, and built an altar under the hill, and twelve pillars, according to the twelve tribes of Israel. And he sent young men of the children of Israel, which offered burnt offerings, and sacrificed peace offerings of oxen unto YeHoVaH. And Moses took half of the blood and put [it] in basons; and half of the blood he sprinkled on the altar. And he took the book of the covenant and read in the audience of the people: and they said, All that YeHoVaH has said will we do, and be obedient. And Moses took the blood, and sprinkled [it] on the people, and said, Behold the blood of the covenant, which YeHoVaH has made with you concerning all these words."

Next, YeHoVaH allowed an entourage of people to come near Him. Together they ate the covenant meal.

> Exodus 24:9-11
> *"Then went up Moses, and Aaron, Nadab, and Abihu, and seventy of the elders of Israel: And they saw the God of Israel: and there was under his feet as it were a paved work of a sapphire stone, and as it were the body of heaven in his clearness. And upon the nobles of the children of Israel he laid not his hand: also, they saw God, and did eat and drink."*

From that point onward, the ketubah (the covenant) became the backbone of the relationship between the two partners, **YeHoVaH and Israel**.

Then, YeHoVaH set in place a safeguard to ensure the covenant passed on to the generations:

> Exodus 24:12
> *Come up to me into the mount and be there: and I will give you tables of stone, and a law, and commandments which I have written; that you may teach them."*

YeHoVaH ensured that Israel as His bride had all she needed. As she walked with Him, in her hands she retained tables of stone[10], the Torah (or instructions), and commandments of YeHoVaH.

---

[10] These Moses broke later, but God restored them to him.

## Chapter 1:
### A Chosen Covenant

While this gave Israel ample information to faithfully serve Him, unfortunately, Israel yielded to a temptation which veered her from her promised exclusivity of serving YeHoVaH. This happened right at the get-go.

*Deuteronomy 9:11-12*
> *"And it came to pass at the end of forty days and forty nights, that YeHoVaH gave me the two tables of stone, even the tables of the covenant. And YeHoVaH said unto me, Arise, get you down quickly from here; for your people which you have brought forth out of Egypt have corrupted themselves; they are quickly turned aside out of the way which I commanded them; they have made them a molten image."*

As Deuteronomy states, Israel corrupted themselves. She made a golden image and worshipped it. In doing so, she broke her covenant commitment to keep herself for YeHoVaH and YeHoVaH alone. In modern terms, when Israel engaged in idolatry, she broke the terms of the ketubah (marriage covenant) and thus, as a result of her unfaithfulness, Israel committed adultery.

Moses, told by YeHoVaH to go down to the people at the base of the mountain, obeys. On his return to the camp, when he sees Israel engaged in the worship of the molten image, he reacts quickly. Immediately, he throws to the ground the two tables of stone written with YeHoVaH's finger, thus breaking them into pieces. This action, although unexpected, prophetically demonstrated to YeHoVaH's people their inability to keep YeHoVaH's commandments.

*Deuteronomy 9:15-19*
> "So, I turned and came down from the mount, and the mount burned with fire: and the two tables of the covenant were in my two hands. And I looked, and behold, you had sinned against YeHoVaH your God and had made you a molten calf: you had turned aside quickly out of the way which YeHoVaH had commanded you. And I took the two tables, and cast them out of my two hands, and brake them before your eyes. And I fell down before YeHoVaH, as at the first, forty days and forty nights: I did neither eat bread, nor drink water, because of all your sins which you sinned, in doing wickedly in the sight of YeHoVaH, to provoke him to anger. For I was afraid of the anger and hot displeasure, wherewith YeHoVaH was wroth against you to destroy you. But YeHoVaH hearkened unto me at that time also."

Israel's actions in breaking her covenant with YeHoVaH put her in danger of being destroyed. A death penalty existed for adultery as well as for a broken blood covenant[11] and the offended party, in this

---

[11] In ancient times, any person(s) who made a blood covenant, in cutting the covenant understood that to break the terms of the

Chapter 1:
A Chosen Covenant

case, YeHoVaH, could demand it. After that scene, Moses rebukes the children of Israel, then returns to the mount. There, Moses fasts forty days and nights before YeHoVaH and intercedes for Israel, also.

YeHoVaH heeds Moses and spares the people the death penalty. Furthermore, YeHoVaH blesses Israel by giving her a sacrificial system, which presented within its pattern, an opportunity to atone for sin. Additionally, while this pattern presents a duplicate of heaven's temple[12], its prophetic picture presents the perfect pattern on how to meet with YeHoVaH and continuously walk with Him. In other words, its pattern prophetically presents God's plan of salvation through Yeshua. In short, its prophetic message within its pattern, *which we call the Mosaic Tabernacle[13]*, showed the only way to life with God is an encounter with Yeshua.

Before leaving this chapter let us summarize ***the basics*** of what we discussed thus far. YeHoVaH, in His infinite wisdom and love, gave to Israel:

---

covenant gave the other(s) member of the covenant agreement the right to kill the ones who broke covenant.

[12] *"And let them make me a sanctuary; that I may dwell among them. According to all that I show you, [after] the pattern of the tabernacle, and the pattern of all the instruments thereof, even so shall you make [it]." Exodus 25:8-9.*

[13] This perfect pattern as seen in the Mosaic Tabernacle we will quickly review in the next chapter.

- *A Blood Covenant* with YeHoVaH comprised of conditions to keep God as their only God, and Israel as God's Covenant people.
- *A Code of Behaviour* outlining YeHoVaH's requirements of Israel, as well as what He would do for Israel, as they obeyed or disobeyed Him.
- *A Penalty of Death* when breaking the covenant.
- *A Sin Offering to make atonement* for breaking the covenant, so they could live and not die.
- *A Unique tabernacle* which spoke prophetically of God in their midst with salvation and the coming Messiah depicted within.

Remember, as God presented this chosen covenant to Israel, it was faultless. However, it had a weakness which did not stem on the side of God, but rather on the side of humankind.

*Romans 8:3*
*"For what the law could not do, in that **it was weak through the flesh**, God sending his own Son in the likeness of sinful flesh, and for sin, condemned sin in the flesh:"*

**As we think of this chosen covenant let us remember it was perfect as God gave it. Its only fault was that its people, apart from God's help, could not perfectly keep it.**

# 2

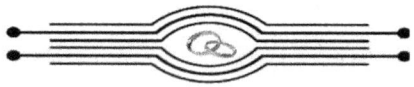

## A Perfect Pattern

*"Now of the things which we have spoken this is the sum: We have such a high priest, who is set on the right hand of the throne of the Majesty in the heavens; A minister of the sanctuary, and of the true tabernacle, which the Lord pitched, and not man. For every high priest is ordained to offer gifts and sacrifices: wherefore it is of necessity that this man have somewhat also to offer. For if he were on earth, he should not be a priest, seeing that there are priests that offer gifts according to the law: Who serve unto the example and shadow of heavenly things, as Moses was admonished of God when he was about to make the tabernacle: for, See, said he, that you make all things according to the pattern showed to you in the mount."*

*Hebrews 8:1-5*

YEHOVAH'S PERFECT PATTERN, as prophetically seen in the tabernacle of Moses, displays the true tabernacle which exists in heaven. In that tabernacle, perfection reigns; however, in the tabernacle on earth, things shift. Reason being sin exists on earth but not in heaven. Therefore, in looking at the perfect pattern of heaven as shown on earth through the Mosaic Tabernacle, and in recognizing the first covenant, we must consider *the effects of the imperfection or sinful nature of humankind*. Due to this weakness (man's tendency to sin), the prophetic picture of the tabernacle and the actual first covenant portrayed that weakness. Paul, the apostle, put it this way:

*Romans 8:3*
*"For what the law could not do, in that it was weak through the flesh, God sending his own Son in the likeness of sinful flesh, and for sin, condemned sin in the flesh:"*

Here, the Bible identifies the weakness as the flesh. God, however, had a perfect solution to overcome that weakness. He sent Yeshua, made in the likeness of sin, but Yeshua never yielded to sin, and thus overcame every evil tendency of the flesh. Therefore, Yeshua lived a perfectly righteous life[14] in all ways, and in doing so, condemned sin in the flesh.

In other words, as we look at the Mosaic Tabernacle, while it prophetically demonstrated the perfect

---

[14] Yeshua never committed as sins of omission or commission but 100% fulfilled God's perfect will.

pattern, it also presented the realization of a need to overcome humankind's sinfulness. This it did, first through its prophetic use of blood sacrifices for sins, which pointed to Yeshua. Then, with its fulfilment at Yeshua's coming.

With His first coming, Yeshua overcame the weakness in the first sacrificial system (first covenant). Through Yeshua, all those who believe in Him and receive Him as their Lord and Saviour, receive His righteousness. Then, as a powerful bonus, His Holy Spirit dwells within the believer, or as scripture calls believers, the temple of the living God.

> 1 Corinthians 3:16
> "Know you not that you are the temple of God, and that the Spirit of God dwells in you?"

In this chapter, as we quickly review the Mosaic Tabernacle, we do so **to show the completion of its prophetic picture regarding Yeshua and God's salvation plan.**

Additionally, three important facts regarding God's perfect pattern for living still applies. These facts are:
1. **Israel's marriage covenant still applies**. This covenant came before that Tabernacle and was never nullified. This means, God still desires Israel as a people to know Him. In addition, the

Torah continues to fulfil its assignment as a school master to bring people to Messiah[15].

2. **Its shadow picture still applies.** Although that unique and specially built tabernacle no longer exists upon this earth, its message still speaks, and its prophetic examples still applies, (e.g. its message of heaven's tabernacle[16], its affirmation to Yeshua as Saviour, and the basics of the believer's life in Messiah, e.g. brazen altar shows redemption, laver sanctification, table of shewbread fellowship, etc.)[17].
3. **Its code of behaviour still applies.** The Torah[18], ten commandments, along with God's precepts, which specify man's behaviour as pleasing to God, still teaches truth.

In summary, the first covenant writings, prophetic shadow pictures and their principles remain of great value. While the tabernacle vanished, the truths which

---

[15] "Wherefore the law was our schoolmaster *to bring us* unto Christ, that we might be justified by faith." *Galatians 3:24*

[16] If you wish to learn more about the Mosaic tabernacle as a pattern of heaven, consider reading or doing a study on "It's All About Heaven". ISBN # Textbook: 978-1-926489-32-2; ISBN # Workbook: 978-1-926489-31-5

[17] *Hebrews 9:1-14*

[18] *"Therefore, by the deeds of the law (Torah) there shall no flesh be justified in his sight: for by the law is the knowledge of sin." Romans 3:20*

they teach still apply. Knowing those truths keeps us free from deception's snare.

## THE MOSAIC TABERNACLE[19]
Let us begin this comparison by walking through the various items shown to us through the tabernacle of Moses. Unfortunately, we only have time to lightly mention these things so this will not be a detailed study. However, our point is to present one specific truth for each of these items. Doing this gives us a little more knowledge which should go a long way to keep us from deception.

### THE GATE/THE FENCE:
In the time of the Mosaic tabernacle, a fence encompassed the tabernacle. There was but one access point: the gate. People, however, could come to a Levitical priest who would teach them the Torah and present offerings and make intercession on their behalf regarding sin.

*TRUTH: One cannot come straight to God. You need to come through the gate, or via His provided entrance.*

---

[19] If you are not familiar with this topic, we suggest you delve into it as soon as you can. There are many wonderful teachings on this subject found on the internet.

*John 14:6*
*"Jesus said unto him, I am the way, the truth, and the life: no man comes unto the Father, but by me."*

**THE BRAZEN ALTAR:**
Here was the place of sacrifice. A priest, ordained by God, presented all offerings, including sin offering. Then, once a year, atonement was made for all people. At that time, the high priest took the blood of the offering, placed it in a basin, and sprinkled it on the mercy seat, first for his own sin, and secondly, for the sin of the people.

**TRUTH**: *Yeshua is the only atonement for sin. He gave Himself as that atonement, once and for all.*

*Hebrews 9:24-26*
*"For Christ is not entered into the holy places made with hands, which are the figures of the true; but into heaven itself, now to appear in the presence of God for us: Nor yet that he should offer himself often, as the high priest enters into the holy place every year with blood of others; For then must he often have suffered since the foundation of the world: but now once in the end of the world has he appeared to put away sin by the sacrifice of himself."*

## Chapter 2:
## A Perfect Pattern

**THE LAVER:**
This laver, made from brass mirrors, reflected the image of the priest. Part of their holiness routine required that they wash before entering the Holy Place and minister before YeHoVaH. Here, we see that Yeshua reflected God or presented YeHoVaH to humankind perfectly.

*TRUTH: A look at Yeshua is to see God. Additionally, believers must reflect the image of the God, Who created them. In other words, God requires that believers be holy as He is holy*[20].

> John 10:30
> "I and my Father are one."

> 2 Timothy 2:19-21
> "Nevertheless, the foundation of God stands sure, having this seal, The Lord knows them that are his. And, let every one that names the name of Christ depart from iniquity. But in a great house there are not only vessels of gold and of silver, but also of wood and of earth; and some to honour, and some to dishonour. If a man therefore purge himself from these, he shall be a vessel unto honour, sanctified, and meet for the master's use, and prepared unto every good work."

---

[20] "Because it is written, Be you holy; for I am holy." *1 Peter 1:16*

## THE HOLY PLACE

As we enter the holy place there are five large pillars which keep the veil in place.

**TRUTH:** *The pillars speak of Yeshua as the Great Shepherd, and the veil speaks of the unity of believers called to walk as one people.*

> Hebrews 13:20-21
> *"Now the God of peace, that brought again from the dead our Lord Jesus, that great shepherd of the sheep, through the blood of the everlasting covenant, Make you perfect in every good work to do his will, working in you that which is well pleasing in his sight, through Jesus Christ; to whom be glory for ever and ever. Amen."*

> 1 Corinthians 1:10
> *"Now I beseech you, brethren, by the name of our Lord Jesus Christ, that you all speak the same thing, and that there be no divisions among you; but that you be perfectly joined together in the same mind and in the same judgment."*

**ROOF:** Above the pillars and the walls lay a covering, which acted as a roof. It contained several layers, the outer one being waterproof.

**TRUTH**: *Amongst its many applications, it speaks about God's protective care of His people, as well as Yeshua, the head who rules over all things, including the church.*

> *Ephesians 1:22*
> *"And has put all things under his feet, and gave him to be the head over all things to the church,"*

## TABLE OF SHEWBREAD
Inside the Holy Place, there sits a table with loaves of bread upon it, one for every tribe.

**TRUTH**: *This speaks of Yeshua as the Bread of Life.*

> *John 6:35*
> *"And Jesus said unto them, I am the bread of life: he that comes to me shall never hunger; and he that believes on me shall never thirst."*

## MENORAH:
The only light within the Holy Place came from the seven-branch menorah. It ran continuously, day and night.

**TRUTH**: *This speaks of Yeshua as the Light of the world.*

> *John 8:12*
> *"Then spake Jesus again unto them, saying, I am the light of the world: he that follows me shall not walk in darkness, but shall have the light of life."*

As Yeshua let His light shine, may believers do the same!

## TABLE OF INCENSE:

Before entering the Holy Holies, there was a veil and the table of incense. Here, incense was presented to God, ignited by the coals from the brazen altar.

**TRUTH**: *Incense speaks of intercession, and this altar of Yeshua's intercessory role.*

> Hebrews 7:25-26
> "Wherefore he is able also to save them to the uttermost all that come unto God by him, seeing he ever lives to make intercession for them. For such a high priest became us, who is holy, harmless, undefiled, separate from sinners, and made higher than the heavens;"

## VEIL BEFORE THE HOLY OF HOLIES

There stood a veil suspended by four large pillars[21]. Upon Yeshua's death, immediately the veil was torn in two from top to bottom.

**TRUTH:** *Through the sacrifice of Yeshua's death, all those who believe on Him as their Lord and Saviour, access God's Presence.*

---

[21] There is much symbolism in these pillars as well as in the many metals and other things which made up the tabernacle. Unfortunately, space does not allow for its investigation.

Chapter 2:
A Perfect Pattern

> *Hebrews 10:19*
> *"Having therefore, brethren, boldness to enter into the holiest by the blood of Jesus, ..."* [22]

## THE ARK OF THE COVENANT

Within the holy of holies rested the Ark of the Covenant. It held the two stones upon which were written the ten commandments. Upon the ark sat the mercy seat upon which the high priest sprinkled the blood on the Day of Atonement.

**TRUTH:** *The Ark of the Covenant represented the holy presence of the living God of all the earth. To stand before Him and not die, one must come through Yeshua. To put it another way, we access God's presence through Yeshua's sacrificial blood sprinkled on the mercy seat. That shed blood speaks of Yeshua's acceptable sacrifice for all mankind and God's pleasure with it.*

Or, in the words of scripture, Yeshua brought about a new and living way to access the presence of God and live!

Repeating and then continuing from the previous scripture:

---

[22] We will continue on with this verse when we discuss the ark, itself.

> *Hebrews 10:19-22*
> *"Having therefore, brethren, boldness to enter into the holiest[23] by the blood of Jesus, By a new and living way, which he has consecrated for us, through the veil, that is to say, his flesh; And having a high priest over the house of God; Let us draw near with a true heart in full assurance of faith, having our hearts sprinkled from an evil conscience, and our bodies washed with pure water."*

Here we end this quick overview of the Mosaic Tabernacle. Unfortunately, it does not even scratch the surface of the subject, however, it does give us enough insight to realize the greatness of what God has done for all humankind through Yeshua. Yeshua stands as God's perfect pattern (or example) to demonstrate the immutable characteristics of God, while at the same time, demonstrates that which God requires of humankind. It also represents God's mercy, as given to sinful man through the life, death, burial and resurrection of Yeshua.

## NEW COVENANT FULFILMENT

Today, we recognize Yeshua as the total fulfilment of God's salvation. He became YeHoVaH's perfect atonement for sin and was the One of whom the prophets spoke. Additionally, once we personally

---

[23] Holy of Holies.

accept Yeshua as our Saviour, we recognize our redemption includes a call to a holy life. Thus, the born-again Christian's life embraces God's call to walk within God's designated holy life. God fully provided for it, and He expects it. Of course, we know to live our life without ever [24]sinning[25], is not possible, but God provides both an advocate and a solution[26] for us.

**DECEPTION AVERTED**

To walk out our life free of deception comes with its challenges but knowing *the basics* God provided for us, teaches us *to discern truth from error*. By referring to the Mt. Sinai experience, its ketubah as well as YeHoVaH's instructions to Israel (torah), we have a good pattern of truth to learn and follow. Above and beyond that, we have the perfect example or perfect pattern of the life of Yeshua.

---

[24] The sum of which includes both sins of commission and omission.

[25] *"If we say that we have no sin, we deceive ourselves, and the truth is not in us. If we confess our sins, he is faithful and just to forgive us our sins, and to cleanse us from all unrighteousness. If we say that we have not sinned, we make him a liar, and his word is not in us."* 1 John 1:8-10.

[26] *"And hereby we do know that we know him, if we keep his commandments. He that said, I know him, and keepeth not his commandments, is a liar, and the truth is not in him. But whoso keepeth his word, in him verily is the love of God perfected: hereby know we that we are in him. He that said he abideth in him ought himself also so to walk, even as he walked."* 1 John 2:3-6

DECEIVED.
How Errors in a Faith System Affect Both God & His People.

YeHoVaH's required code of behaviour as given in the torah[27], (the instructions of God) which include the ten commandments, give us facts to check against any lures or baits set out to deceive. A solid knowledge of these things prepares us well for our battle against deception. In fact, we can use these basic elements of the faith as a powerful check list against deception.

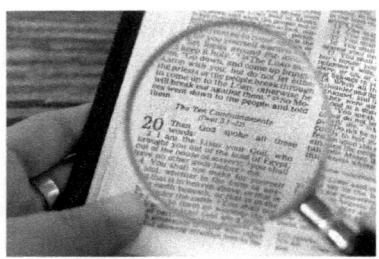

Just as in banking, knowing *the original* gives one the best advantage of spotting *the counterfeit*. As believers study the Word of God, learn its commandments and precepts, and with that information[28], understand the requirements of God, they protect themselves from deception.

As promised in the introduction, we have laid out the basics, which included tangible facts with which students of the Word can use to fight deception. While

---

[27] Remember, the Torah, KJV interprets as the Law really means instructions of God.

[28] This book is written from the mindset that the New Covenant does not excuse believers from obeying the commandments of God, nor grasping His ways, which include understanding the precepts presented in the first (old) covenant.

deception can be tricky, the tangible facts act as good evidence to the discerning person. Then, in the next section as we move forward to look at patterns of deception, we will examine ways in which deception decorates its traps and snares to mislead, misdirect and misalign the unsuspecting.

**BEFORE CLOSING THIS CHAPTER**
Dear reader, please ensure that you know, understand, and have a grasp of *the original, namely Yeshua Ha' Mashiach*. In other words, please ensure that you are a genuine believer[29], and that you know, first hand, **the basic foundational beliefs[30] of the Christian faith,** especially the ones shown in this chapter. Knowledge of these go a long way to safeguard against deception.

With regards to the covenant with God, or regarding the many lessons within the Tabernacle of Moses, if you are not familiar with them, please consider strengthening your knowledge of this as time goes on. Remember, understanding the shadow picture of Yeshua, as **revealed within the tabernacle of Moses,**

---

[29] If you are not sure, please read Salvation's Message in the Appendix.
[30] As we walked through the Mosaic Tabernacle, we presented aspects of the Christian faith such as Yeshua as the only way to life, and Yeshua, the perfect mirror of human behaviour, etc.

will fortify and equip you with a powerful understanding of God's intentions for your life.

*Father, please help every one of us to grasp, understand and grow in our knowledge of the commands, precepts, concepts and covenants of God. Help us to know You and Your ways! In doing so, may we become fortified and wise to deception and its tactics and thus, learn to avert it on every front.*

*Amen*

Dear Reader:

As you proceed to study biblical patterns which indicate deception, please remember to think about some earlier mentions of God's Perfect Pattern, Yeshua. Look at **the heart** of the call of God to human beings, as well as the Way that He prepared for them to walk. Of that walk, Yeshua said:

*"Enter you in at the strait gate: for wide is the gate, and broad is the way, that leads to destruction, and many there be which go in thereat: Because strait is the gate, and narrow is the way, which leads unto life, and few there be that find it. Beware of false prophets, which come to you in sheep's clothing, but inwardly they are ravening wolves. You shall know them by their fruits ..."*

*Matthew 7:13-16*

While that walk begins as a narrow way and continues to be so the more you walk in it, the presence of God and His rewards are well worth it.

*"Be strong and of a good courage, fear not, nor be afraid of them: for YeHoVaH your God, he it is that does go with you; he will not fail you, nor forsake you."*

*Deuteronomy 31:6*

# 3

## A Shrouded Scheme

*"And I will set your bounds from the Red sea even unto the sea of the Philistines, and from the desert unto the river: for I will deliver the inhabitants of the land into your hand; and you shall drive them out before you. You shall make no covenant with them, nor with their gods. They shall not dwell in your land, lest they make you sin against me: for if you serve their gods, it will surely be a snare unto you."*

*Exodus 23:31-33*

**D**URING THEIR TIME in the wilderness and again, right before the people of Israel entered Canaan land, they received a warning from YeHoVaH through Moses.

*Deuteronomy 7:2-6*
  *"And when YeHoVaH your God shall deliver them (the enemy) before you; you shall smite them, and utterly*

*destroy them; you shall make no covenant with them, nor show mercy unto them: Neither shall you make marriages with them; your daughter you shall not give unto his son, nor his daughter shall you take unto your son. For they will turn away your son from following me, that they may serve other gods: so will the anger of YeHoVaH be kindled against you and destroy you suddenly. But thus, shall you deal with them; you shall destroy their altars, and break down their images, and cut down their groves, and burn their graven images with fire. For you are a holy people unto YeHoVaH your God: YeHoVaH your God has chosen you to be a special people unto himself, above all people that are upon the face of the earth.[31]"*

This passage included some warnings given in the Torah, along with reasons to obey.

1. **Do not make a covenant** with the people of the land.
2. **Do not marry them** for they will turn you from serving Me that you may serve other gods. Then YeHoVaH's anger will kindle against you, and He shall suddenly destroy you.[32]

---

[31] This admonition they received before entering Canaan land. Another warning came in Exodus 23:31-33

[32] Remember the penalty for broken blood covenants was death demanded by the offending party. If a broken covenant existed,

## Chapter 3:
## A Shrouded Scheme

Alongside of what the Torah forbad, came instructions of what God expected of His people and why. This is how God told Israel to deal with the traps and snares set before them[33]:

**INSTRUCTIONS:**
1. Destroy their altars.
2. Break down their images.
3. Cut down their groves.
4. Burn their graven images with fire.

**REASONS WHY:**
1. You are a holy people unto YeHoVaH.
2. You are a chosen people, special to YeHoVaH, above all people upon the face of the earth.

At this point, we will look at the Hebrew word for holy:

| Strong's # | Hebrew word: holy | Pronunciation |
|---|---|---|
| 6944 | קֹדֶשׁ | qodesh (ko'-desh) |
| Interpreted as holy, something set apart. | | |

---

meaning the person no longer walked with YeHoVaH, then no atonement existed for their sin and death resulted. See Hebrews 10:29 for application for today.

[33] These actions leave no stumbling block behind nor gives occasion for the enemy to arise in that place.

# DECEIVED.
### How Errors in a Faith System Affect Both God & His People.

In the Hebrew picture language, the meaning of this word comes to life. It is as follows:

| Hebrew Word: Holy | | קָדוֹשׁ | |
|---|---|---|---|
| **Parent Root:** | | | |
| ק | Sun on horizon | Tomorrow, that which comes from above, or something in its beginning, etc. | |
| ד | Tent door | Door, doorway, entrance way, gate, etc. | |
| Parent Root Picture | | That which comes from above and enters in. | |
| **Child Root[34]** | | | |
| ו | nail | Attach, secure, join, enjoin, etc. | |
| שׁ | Two front teeth | Destroy, devour, separate, overcome, conquer, etc. | |
| Child Root Picture | | Enjoins to separate or removing. | |
| **Overall Meaning** | | | |
| That which comes from above enters to enjoin itself and destroy. | | | |

Through this pictograph language we see a deeper meaning of the word holy. It shows that God, the One from above, comes, and enjoining Himself to a person,

---

[34] Most people add the vav to make the Hebrew word for holy.

## Chapter 3:
## A Shrouded Scheme

devours that which is not like Him. With this word, therefore, we see the reason why God calls His people to a holy life. It is so that we can be like Him, or in other words, return to the image He created in humankind in the garden.

*Genesis 1:27*
*"So, God created man in his own image, in the image of God created he him; male and female created he them."*

If God's people turn from the covenant made with God, then *instead of opening a door to God* to draw near them and bring them to a place of holiness so they reflect Him image, *they open a door to that which destroys them.* That is one more reason why YeHoVaH ordered the destruction of every altar, molten image and grove dedicated to false gods. This aspect we see when comparing the pictograph meaning of the word, קָדֵשׁ Holy, to the pictograph meaning of the word for unclean, טָמֵא.

| Strong's # | Hebrew word Unclean | Pronunciation |
|---|---|---|
| 2931 | טָמֵא | tame' taw-may' |
| Interpreted as unclean, or impure. | | |

# DECEIVED.
## How Errors in a Faith System Affect Both God & His People.

| Hebrew Word: Unclean | טָמֵא |
|---|---|
| **Parent Root:** | |
| טֻ | Snake in a basket | Hidden, womb, surround, contain, snare, plot, lie in wait, to deceive |
| מֵ | Waters of the sea | Waters of life, chaos, unstable, oppressive and more |
| *Parent Root Picture* | *Plot or snare to bring chaos.* |
| **Child Root**[35] | |
| א | Ox head | Strong leader, first leader, strong, powerful, pulling. |
| *Child Root Picture* | *Becomes the strong leader* |
| **Overall Meaning** That which hides, plots to snare, trap or bring chaos and that becomes the leading force. | |

It is no wonder that the Torah, (God's Instructions) forbad God's people from embracing *the unclean thing*. Its purpose comes to destroy. Therefore, no covenants of any kind, especially in a marriage where two become one with them, would be beneficial or profitable.

With this background, let us investigate an early time in Israel's history when the man Balaam served as a prophet.

---

[35] Most people add the vav to make the Hebrew word for holy.

Chapter 3:
A Shrouded Scheme

## BALAAM AND KING BALAK

Numbers, Chapter 22 opens with the location of the children of Israel. Moses was still with them as they camped in the plains of Moab near the Jordan River. Numbers further tell us that the Israelites grew great in number, and so much so that the King of the Moabites, Balak, feared them. Balak became very distressed over their presence in his land and thus, he sought for a solution to destroy them.

## BALAK'S SOLUTION

YeHoVaH blessed the Israelites, *but* king Balak reasoned that if he could persuade a prophet to curse the Israelites in the name of YeHoVaH and thus remove them from God's favour, then his problem of God's protective hand over Israel would end. Balak, therefore, sought out a prophet for hire, named Balaam. Balaam, according to scripture had encounters with YeHoVaH. However, with each encounter God warns Balaam not to curse Israel.

*Numbers 22:12*
   *"And God said unto Balaam, You shall not go with them; you shall not curse the people: for they are blessed."*

*Numbers 23:7-10*
   *"And he took up his parable, and said, Balak the king of Moab has brought me from Aram, out of the mountains of the east, [saying], Come, curse me Jacob, and come,*

*defy Israel. How shall I curse, whom God has not cursed? or how shall I defy, [whom] YeHoVaH has not defied? For from the top of the rocks I see him, and from the hills I behold him: lo, the people shall dwell alone and shall not be reckoned among the nations. Who can count the dust of Jacob, and the number of the fourth [part] of Israel? Let me die the death of the righteous and let my last end be like his!"*

Frustrated, King Balak continues to pursue Balaam to curse Israel.

*Numbers 23:17-24*

*"And when he came to him, behold, he stood by his burnt offering, and the princes of Moab with him. And Balak said unto him, What has YeHoVaH spoken? And he took up his parable, and said, Rise up, Balak, and hear; listen unto me, you son of Zippor: God [is] not a man, that he should lie; neither the son of man, that he should repent: has he said, and shall he not do [it]? or has he spoken, and shall he not make it good? Behold, I have received [commandment] to bless: and he has blessed; and I cannot reverse it. He has not beheld iniquity in Jacob, neither has he seen perverseness in Israel: YeHoVaH his God [is] with him, and the shout of a king [is] among them. God brought them out of Egypt; he has as it were the strength of an unicorn. Surely [there is] no enchantment against Jacob, neither [is there] any divination against Israel: according to*

## Chapter 3:
## A Shrouded Scheme

*this time it shall be said of Jacob and of Israel, What has God wrought! Behold, the people shall rise up as a great lion, and lift up himself as a young lion: he shall not lie down until he eat [of] the prey, and drink the blood of the slain."*

Balak, becoming increasingly annoyed with Balaam, nevertheless, tries again:

*Numbers 24:2-9*
"And Balaam lifted up his eyes, and he saw Israel abiding [in his tents] according to their tribes; and the spirit of God came upon him. And he took up his parable, and said, Balaam the son of Beor has said, and the man whose eyes are open has said: He has said, which heard the words of God, which saw the vision of the Almighty, falling [into a trance], but having his eyes open: How goodly are your tents, O Jacob, [and] your tabernacles, O Israel! As the valleys are they spread forth, as gardens by the river's side, as the trees of lign aloes which YeHoVaH has planted, [and] as cedar trees beside the waters. He shall pour the water out of his buckets, and his seed [shall be] in many waters, and his king shall be higher than Agag, and his kingdom shall be exalted. God brought him forth out of Egypt; he has as it were the strength of an unicorn: he shall eat up the nations his enemies, and shall break their bones, and pierce [them] through with his arrows. He couched, he lay down as a lion, and as a great lion:

*who shall stir him up? Blessed [is] he that blesses you, and cursed [is] he that curses you."*

After this, the king becomes furious with Balaam. Nevertheless, Balaam does not curse Israel. While he does give a prophetic word which speaks of the Messiah, and never prophetically curses Israel, Balaam betrays Israel with the counsel he gives the king.

*Numbers 31:16*
*"Behold, these caused the children of Israel, through the counsel of Balaam, to commit trespass against YeHoVaH in the matter of Peor, and there was a plague among the congregation of YeHoVaH."*

While we do not have one passage outlining Balaam's advice, we know the results: **to commit trespass against YeHoVaH.** Additionally, we have a text in numbers which gives us more information.

*Numbers 25:1-2*
*"And Israel abode in Shittim, and the people began to commit whoredom with the daughters of Moab. And they called the people unto the sacrifices of their gods: and the people did eat, and bowed down to their gods."*

## Chapter 3:
## A Shrouded Scheme

Although Balaam did not curse Israel for the king of Moab, he gave counsel which, when followed, corrupted Israel. Balaam's counsel, very simply, introduced unclean things into Israel. Israel, obviously not following the Torah's advice, entered into sexual union with the Moabite women (with or without marriage covenants), enjoyed their sacrifices to false gods with them, and eventually bowed to their gods.

In reviewing Balaam's counsel to the king of Moad, we see it results. If it had been advice to go to war, Israel may have taken up arms and destroyed them. Balaam's counsel was a scheme shrouded in deception, one which appealed to the flesh, or else the Bible puts it, loving the world.

*1 John 2:15-17*
*"Love not the world, neither the things that are in the world. If any man love the world, the love of the Father is not in him. For all that is in the world, the lust of the flesh, and the lust of the eyes, and the pride of life, is not of the Father, but is of the world. And the world passes away, and the lust thereof: but he that does the will of God abides for ever."*

Just like the gate around the tabernacle of Moses fenced out the world from crashing in on the sacred things of God, so a believer holds to the guidelines of scripture to ensure the world and its mindset does not overtake them.

> *James 4:4*
> *"You adulterers and adulteresses, know you not that the friendship of the world is enmity with God? whosoever therefore will be a friend of the world is the enemy of God."*

Additionally, the New Covenant gives us a warning regarding Balaam like characters. Speaking about false prophets, it says:

> *2 Peter 2:14-16*
> *"Having eyes full of adultery, and that cannot cease from sin; beguiling unstable souls: an heart they have exercised with covetous practices; cursed children: Which have forsaken the right way, and are gone astray, following the way of Balaam the son of Bosor, who loved the wages of unrighteousness[36]; But was rebuked for his iniquity: the dumb ass speaking with man's voice forbad the madness of the prophet."*

As we close out this chapter, let us consider the ways of Balaam and his counsel. While, according to

---

[36] While we are not specifically told in the first covenant scripture that Balaam sold out to the king, Peter, in his message regarding false prophets declares that Balaam got paid for his counsel.

scripture he met with YeHoVaH, heard Him and spoke for Him, his heart within him lacked integrity. His actions showed that he did not love God with all his being, *nor his neighbour as himself.* If he had done the latter, he would never have given the king of Moab fodder to destroy Israel.

Additionally, let each of us consider our heart before God to ensure our hearts are sold out to Him, and that we do not love the world, what it offers, nor its call to deny God or His principles for living, such as to love our neighbour as ourselves.

Dear one, let us remember this saying, based on a summary of Yeshua's words in John 17:14-16 and John 15:19:

*"Be in the world, but not a part of it".*

**Lord, please give us eyes for You, alone and wisdom to recognize and then expose deception's every shrouded scheme.**

# 4

## A Destined Disaster

*"And Jesus answered and said unto them, Take heed that no man deceive you. For many shall come in my name, saying, I am Christ; and shall deceive many."*

Matthew 24:4-5

AS YESHUA SPOKE OF END TIMES, He answered His disciples' question: *"What shall the sign be when all these things shall be fulfilled?"* Yeshua explained about wars and rumours of wars and other things which shall happen before His return. Yet, as we review His words, we often overlook one sign, namely, His *first* warning sign:

**"Take heed that no man deceive you".**

Taking His warning under advisement, we note that deception, like the other warning signs Yeshua gave, exponentially increases the closer we come to His return. In other words, deception's ability to deceive *increases in frequency, depth and intensity the closer we come to the timeframe of Yeshua's return.*

> Matthew 24:24-25
> "For there shall arise false Christs, and false prophets, and shall show great signs and wonders; insomuch that, if it were possible, they shall deceive the very elect. Behold, I have told you before."

In Yeshua's message He speaks of deception's tactics and the various forms in which it takes[37]. From His teachings we deduce that deception's persuasive abilities own a driving force which aims its sights to deceive the very elect. Yet, the elect *(God's true followers), if* they heed Yeshua's warnings, will be awake and ready. Therefore, every believer must embrace Yeshua's warning, hopefully with gratefulness for it since it came beforehand, giving us ample time *to fortify our defences.*

Yeshua's words, "take heed", then, stand as a call to awareness, a call to being prepared, as well as a call to action. In other words, His warnings stand as a command to watch[38].

---

[37] *Read Matthew 24:4-51.*
[38] *"Take you heed, watch and pray: for you know not when the time is." Mark 13:33.*

## Chapter 4:
## A Destined Disaster

Deception masquerades as something good yet it is sinister. It pretends to be good, while in its depth, it is anything but good. We see that in the Hebrew word for deceive.

It is the word נָשָׁא [39].

| Strong's # | Hebrew word: Deceive | Pronunciation |
|---|---|---|
| 5377 | נָשָׁא | nasha' naw-shaw' |
| Normally interpreted as deceive or beguiled | | |

| Hebrew Word: Deceive | | נָשָׁא |
|---|---|---|
| **Parent Root:** | | |
| בּ | seed | Heir, life which continues, inheritance, offspring. |
| שָׁ | Two front teeth | To devour, destroy, consume, tear to pieces, conquer, etc. |
| Parent Root Picture | | *Receiving that which devours or destroys.* |

---

[39] In researching this word online, it became apparent that some people do not think Strong's attributed this word correctly. However, in researching the matter in ancient manuscripts online, it is the author's conclusion that Strong's is correct. See https://biblehub.com/text/isaiah/19-13.htm for one example.

| Child Root | | |
|---|---|---|
| א | Ox head | Strong leader, first leader, strong, powerful, pulling. |
| *Child Root Picture* | | *Becomes the strong leader* |
| **Overall Meaning** | | |
| That, which one receives which in turn destroys or devours. It becomes the strong leader or in other words, it becomes first in the person's life. | | |

Using this information, one cautiously looks at deception knowing that it brings with it an agenda. In the end, that agenda devours or destroys what previously existed. Then, it lives in the place formerly occupied putting itself in first place.

This possible word picture meaning fits well within the parameters of Yeshua's warning. Remember, He called us *to a proactive approach*, to watch, to be aware of deception. To embrace His advice in the deepest sense, we must recognize that deception carries with it a destructive, even deadly agenda, one which intends to contradict God's basic instruction for living.

Never should we allow deception to have a place in our life! If, as believers, we desire to avert deception's traps, we must be alert and examine **the facts**, looking for **the fake**, and then, reject it. Furthermore, we must go beyond weighing things alongside our own mindsets, putting aside our own measuring stick! We

## Chapter 4:
## A Destined Disaster

must have another measuring stick, that of *God's Word*[40].

If we fail to examine philosophies, teachings or other things presented to us, **comparing their content to the heart of the Word of God**, we leave ourselves unguarded. Yes, *failure to measure all things against God's Word* is a dangerous mindset. Such a mindset easily convinces one to simply sit back and give deception opportunity. If that mindset continues and one adjusts their views accordingly, deception becomes the norm. In the end, truth escapes one's reality.

That was deception's pattern throughout the book of Judges. At that time in Israel's history, people set their own moral compass. The bottom line to that mindset suggests that human beings know better than God. Such thinking gives deception persuasion advantage. ***No, No, No! A thousand times No!*** Rather, let the history recorded in God's Word speak to us loud and clear. Let us learn to watch, to be on guard against deception. Let us in engrave Yeshua's warning upon our minds and let us ***"take heed"***.

---

[40] Remember, too, that it is in *the Hebrew transcripts* that we must search, not in any modern translation where the possibility exists for humanism or other "isms" to add its opinion.

So, as we walk through this lesson, which includes insights on the book of Judges, let us learn well from the timeframe under discussion in Israel's history. Let us learn to recognize the warning in Judges. It comes by way of a major theme within the book, summarized by this key phrase:

> "every man did that which was right in his own eyes".

Once we recognize this attitude, we can avoid following their example set in the book of Judges.

## ISRAEL DURING THE BOOK OF JUDGES

As the Torah closes, the book of Joshua begins. During the time of Joshua, we see Israel's attempt to walk in obedience to God and thus enjoy a great victory[41]. As long as Israel obeyed God, she won her battles. As the book Joshua closes, we read:

*Joshua 24:31*
*"And Israel served YeHoVaH all the days of Joshua, and all the days of the elders that outlived Joshua, and which had known all the works of YeHoVaH, that he had done for Israel."*

---

[41] Israel encountered a problem with the battle at Ai. A man names, Achan, out of greed, took and hid forbidden property in his tent. This action caused Israel defeat at Ai. We will discuss later in this book.

## Chapter 4:
## A Destined Disaster

After Joshua, we encounter the book of Judges, when Israel walked in disobedience to God. As a result, God, gave them over to their enemies who oppressed them.

> *Judges 2:14-15*
> *"And the anger of YeHoVaH was hot against Israel, and he delivered them into the hands of spoilers that spoiled them, and he sold them into the hands of their enemies round about, so that they could not any longer stand before their enemies. Whithersoever they went out, the hand of YeHoVaH was against them for evil, as YeHoVaH had said, and as YeHoVaH had sworn unto them: and they were greatly distressed."*

God, in His mercy, raised up judges, anointed leaders, to lead and guide Israel. Yet, their time in leadership seemed like a band-aid solution due to the stubbornness of the people who refused to consistently obey God. As each judge ruled, Israel repented and then enjoyed victory, but after that judge died, the people returned to their old ways and their enemies oppressed them once again. Throughout the entire book of Judges, we see a cycle where Israel cried out to God, repented, and received their deliverer; then, after the deliverer died they returned to corruption.

> *Judges 2:16-19*
> *"Nevertheless, YeHoVaH raised up judges, which delivered them out of the hand of those that spoiled them. And yet they would not listen unto their judges,*

> *but they went a whoring after other gods and bowed themselves unto them: they turned quickly out of the way which their fathers walked in, obeying the commandments of YeHoVaH; [but] they did not so. And when YeHoVaH raised them up judges, then YeHoVaH was with the judge, and delivered them out of the hand of their enemies all the days of the judge: for it repented YeHoVaH because of their groanings by reason of them that oppressed them and vexed them. And it came to pass, when the judge was dead, [that] they returned, and corrupted [themselves] more than their fathers, in following other gods to serve them, and to bow down unto them; they ceased not from their own doings, nor from their stubborn way."*

Israel's bottom line *in not serving God*, verse 19 captures for us:

> Judges 2:19
> "And it came to pass, when the judge was dead, that they returned, and corrupted themselves more than their fathers, in following other gods to serve them, and to bow down unto them; **they ceased not from their own doings, nor from their stubborn way.**"

Yes, this cycle repeats itself. As the book of Judges ends, it summarizes the entire years of Israel before they requested a king from God.

# Chapter 4:
## A Destined Disaster

> *Judges 21:24-25*
> *"And the children of Israel departed from there at that time, every man to his tribe and to his family, and they went out from there every man to his inheritance. In those days there was no king in Israel: every man did that which was right in his own eyes."*

About the time that Samuel, Israel's last judge, comes on the scene, Israel sees her problem from a different perspective than God. Israel believes their oppression came because the other nations perceived them as weak, because they did not have a king over them, like the other nations. Therefore, Israel thought that if she had a king, her problems would end.

As Samuel grows older and is ready to die, they call upon Samuel to intercede for them and ask God to give them a king.

> *1 Samuel 12:19-25*
> *"And all the people said unto Samuel, Pray for your servants unto YeHoVaH your God, that we die not: for we have added unto all our sins this evil, to ask us a king. And Samuel said unto the people, Fear not: you have done all this wickedness: yet turn not aside from following YeHoVaH, but serve YeHoVaH with all your heart; And turn you not aside: for then should you go after vain things, which cannot profit nor deliver; for they are vain. For YeHoVaH will not forsake his people*

*for his great name's sake: because it has pleased YeHoVaH to make you his people. Moreover as for me, God forbid that I should sin against YeHoVaH in ceasing to pray for you: but I will teach you the good and the right way: Only fear YeHoVaH, and serve him in truth with all your heart: for consider how great things he has done for you. But if you shall still do wickedly, you shall be consumed, both you and your king.*

From this passage, it becomes clear that Israel followed things which neither profited them nor gave them victory. Samuel longed to see that change. Indeed, he preferred they follow after YeHoVaH with all their heart and encouraged them to do so.

## THE TABERNACLE OF MOSES

During the time of Judges, the tabernacle of Moses experienced corruption problems as the service to YeHoVaH degenerated[42]. God warned the high priest in charge of the Mosaic Tabernacle, Eli, that He would not tolerate the despicable behaviour by Eli's sons. As Eli aged, his sons would not take his place but rather, they would die[43]. On the day when God fulfilled His

---

[42] 1 *Samuel 2:17; 24;*
[43] God rose up Samuel to carry on, however, by the time he took office after Eli's death, the tabernacle was no longer in place.

Chapter 4:
A Destined Disaster

Word to Eli, his two sons died. When Eli heard the news, he died also.

Yet, along with those circumstances, something even more tragic happened. Through a series of incidents, the enemy captured the Ark of the Covenant. It was in enemy territory for seven months[44], then returned to Israel. In the meantime, Israel's other enemies raided and burned to the ground the Tabernacle of Moses. They left nothing behind except ashes and the stone foundation upon which they set the tabernacle[45]. So, as the nation entered the time of the kings, they did so without the Tabernacle of Moses, and without Samuel, too.

On the national scene, Israel stood in a waiting mode as David awaited in the background for his time as king.

**DECEPTION'S DESTINED DISASTER**
This time in Israel teaches us the horrible price that Israel paid for walking away from their covenant partner, YeHoVaH, to serve other gods. We recognize their absence of the Torah and note that only some

---

[44] *1 Samuel 6:1*
[45] It is believed that Shiloh in Israel, today, shows the remaining stones from this time.

individuals walked within its principles[46]. It appears its message did not reach the hearts of most of Israel. Instead, they did wickedly in the sight of their God. Israel lost their moral compass, and every person continued to do what they thought was right in their own eyes.

According to the Bible, only God is righteous in all His ways.

> *Psalm 145:17*
> *"The LORD [is] righteous in all his ways, and holy in all his works."*

Regarding the ways of human beings, which one of us do no iniquity and walk in all of God's ways one hundred percent of the time? It is, however, the Psalmist prayer to God to help us do so:

> *Psalm 119:1-8*
> *"ALEPH. Blessed [are] the undefiled in the way, who walk in the law of YeHoVaH. Blessed [are] they that keep his testimonies, [and that] seek him with the whole heart. They also do no iniquity: they walk in his ways."*
>
> *"You have commanded [us] to keep your precepts diligently. O that my ways were directed to keep your*

---

[46] Samuel's mother and father and Samuel did, as did some others than are not named.

## Chapter 4:
## A Destined Disaster

*statutes! Then shall I not be ashamed, when I have respect unto all your commandments."*

*"I will praise you with uprightness of heart, when I shall have learned your righteous judgments. I will keep your statutes: O forsake me not utterly."*

Only Yeshua walked in all God's ways, never failing Him, once. As believers walking with God, although we do our best to know His ways and walk in them, we must remember the apostle John's word to us:

1 John 1:8-10
"If we say that we have no sin, we deceive ourselves, and the truth is not in us. If we confess our sins, he is faithful and just to forgive us our sins, and to cleanse us from all unrighteousness. If we say that we have not sinned, we make him a liar, and his word is not in us."

Believers cannot afford to measure things by doing that which is right in our own eyes. Rather, our motto must be to do that which in right in God's eyes.

As we end this lesson, let us remember that scripture witnesses to the great defeat which came to the nation of Israel whenever they forsook God to serve other gods. They paid a painful penalty whenever they set aside His commands and precepts, preferring to implement their own measuring stick for right and wrong. These tactics of deception convinced Israel that she knew better than God!

## DECEIVED.
### How Errors in a Faith System Affect Both God & His People.

Oh, how great is deception's mantle! How sinister its goal, to convince and deceive so many! Therefore, let each one of us take a lesson from the mistakes of those who have gone before us. Let us be intent on following the ways of God, ensuring that we measure our thoughts, words, deeds, and beliefs against the Word of God. Furthermore, let us ensure that we invite the searchlight of the Holy Spirit to search our heart and thus discern our intent. In the words of King David let us pray:

> *Psalm 139:23-24*
> *"Search me, O God, and know my heart: try me, and know my thoughts: And see if there be any wicked way in me, and lead me in the way everlasting."*

Additionally, let us treasure and cling to the Word of God, embracing its wisdom. Let us ensure that God's Word, precepts and commands frame our moral compass. Moreover, let us take heed and mark well Yeshua's warnings, including this one:

> *Mark 4:9*
> *"And he said unto them, He that has ears to hear, let him hear."*

**In doing so, let us escape deception's snare, and thus, avert its destined disaster!**

# 5

## *A Deceptive Devotion*

*"But YeHoVaH [is] the true God, he [is] the living God, and an everlasting king: at his wrath the earth shall tremble, and the nations shall not be able to abide his indignation."*

Jeremiah 10:10

**K**INGS OF EARTH RULE over a parcel of the earth, but YeHoVaH rules to the ends of the earth. Kings of earth reign for a season, but YeHoVaH's term of office never ends. Earthly kings die and leave their throne to another, but no one dethrones YeHoVaH! When He arises from His throne to execute His judgments and to judge the earth, the earth trembles before Him. Indeed, every nation under heaven shakes as YeHoVaH arises to judge the earth.

Indeed, earthly kings, mere mortals with flesh and bone, reign for limited time spans and with limited power. Known to some kings, as the Divine Right of kings, some kings make judgments cognitive of God and their responsibility to Him. Others care not to give accountability to God and thus, put themselves in the place of God.

Nevertheless, the reign of each king leaves behind a legacy written with the indelible ink of history's pen. As the Bible writes with its pen, it records God's perspective. It either gives God's stamp of approval on a Godly, fair and just reign, or expresses its rejection for ungodly kings who refuse to comply with God's standards. Comments such as these, the Bible recorded about the reign of King Saul of Israel.

> *1 Chronicles 10:13-14*
> *"So Saul died for his transgression which he committed against YeHoVaH, [even] against the word of YeHoVaH, which he kept not, and also for asking [counsel] of [one that had] a familiar spirit[47], to enquire [of it]; And inquired not of YeHoVaH: therefore he slew him, and turned the kingdom unto David the son of Jesse."*

In this overview of Saul's life, the Bible emphasized Saul's transgressions against the laws of God. It stressed his inability to keep God's Word. In addition, it chronicled his actions to seek counsel from an unauthorized source, namely the witch[48] of Endor[49].

---

[47] A witch.
[48] One with a familiar spirit.
[49] *1 Samuel 28:7*

## Chapter 5:
## A Deceptive Devotion

With Saul's reign degenerated to that degree, God removed Saul from his royal throne and turned the kingdom over to David, the son of Jesse. Yet, Saul, began his reign as the hope of Israel.

Immediately prior to Saul's appointment as King, Samuel, the prophet, was aging and his prophetic career about to end. Israel did not want another judge over them, especially one of Samuel's sons. So, the people of Israel came to Samuel saying, "Give us a king!"

> *1 Samuel 8:4-5*
> *"Then all the elders of Israel gathered themselves together, and came to Samuel unto Ramah, And said unto him, Behold, you are old, and your sons walk not in your ways: now make us a king to judge us like all the nations."*

Samuel, reluctant and rejected, presented the petition to YeHoVaH. Afterward, YeHoVaH told Samuel not to take it personally. Israel did not reject Samuel, the prophet, but rather they rejected YeHoVaH as their king.

> *1 Samuel 8:6-9*
> *But the thing displeased Samuel, when they said, Give us a king to judge us. And Samuel prayed unto YeHoVaH. And YeHoVaH said unto Samuel, Listen*

*unto the voice of the people in all that they say unto you: for they have not rejected you, but they have rejected me, that I should not reign over them. According to all the works which they have done since the day that I brought them up out of Egypt even unto this day, wherewith they have forsaken me, and served other gods, so do they also unto you. Now therefore listen unto their voice: nevertheless, yet protest solemnly unto them, and show them the manner of the king that shall reign over them.*

Following God's instructions, Samuel gathers the people together. Protesting to them regarding their choice to demand a king, Samuel outlined Israel's future life under a king:

This will be the type of king that shall reign over you:
- He will take your sons and appoint them to serve in his army[50].

---

[50] 1 Samuel 8:11-12 *"And he said, This will be the manner of the king that shall reign over you: He will take your sons, and appoint them for himself, for his chariots, and to be his horsemen; and some shall run before his chariots. And he will appoint him captains over thousands, and captains over fifties; and will set them to ear his ground, and to reap his harvest, and to make his instruments of war, and instruments of his chariots."*

## Chapter 5:
## A Deceptive Devotion

- He will take your daughters to prepare food for himself and his army[51].
- He will take your fields, and your vineyards, and your olive yards, even the best of them, and give them to his servants[52].
- He will take the tenth of your seed, and of your vineyards, and give to his officers, and to his servants[53].
- And he will take your menservants, and your maidservants, and your goodliest young men, and your donkeys, and put them to his work[54].
- He will take the tenth of your sheep: and
- You shall be his servants[55]

Samuel warned them, that when these things happened, they would cry out to YeHoVaH because of the King they chose. However, Samuel continued, YeHoVaH would not hear them in that day[56].

Nevertheless, the people insisted on their own way.

---

[51] 1 Samuel 8:13 *"And he will take your daughters to be confectionaries, and to be cooks, and to be bakers."*
[52] 1 Samuel 8:14
[53] 1 Samuel 8:15
[54] 1 Samuel 8:16
[55] 1 Samuel 8:17
[56] 1 Samuel 8:18

*1 Samuel 8:19-20*

*"Nevertheless, the people refused to obey the voice of Samuel; and they said, Nay; but we will have a king over us; That we also may be like all the nations; and that our king may judge us, and go out before us, and fight our battles."*

So, God gave them King Saul. In stature, he was tall, almost giant like in size, being from the shoulders upward, higher than any of the people[57]. Immediately thereafter, God sent them into battle, a battle which they won.

*1 Samuel 15:7-9*

*"And Saul smote the Amalekites from Havilah [until] you come to Shur, that [is] over against Egypt. And he took Agag the king of the Amalekites alive, and utterly destroyed all the people with the edge of the sword. But Saul and the people spared Agag, and the best of the sheep, and of the oxen, and of the fatlings, and the lambs, and all [that was] good, and would not utterly destroy them: but every thing [that was] vile and refuse, that they destroyed utterly."*

---

[57] *1 Samuel 10:23 "And they ran and fetched him thence: and when he stood among the people, he was higher than any of the people from his shoulders and upward."*

## Chapter 5:
## A Deceptive Devotion

Saul only partially obeyed his orders from YeHoVaH. He kept the best of the sheep, oxen, fatlings and lambs and all that was good. He also allowed the King of the Amalekites, Agag[58], to live, a thing which God did not desire.

> *1 Samuel 15:10-12*
>
> *"Then came the word of YeHoVaH unto Samuel, saying, It repents[59] me that I have set up Saul [to be] king: for he is turned back from following me, and has not performed my commandments. And it grieved Samuel; and he cried unto YeHoVaH all night. And when Samuel rose early to meet Saul in the morning, it was told Samuel, saying, Saul came to Carmel, and, behold, he set him up a place, and is gone about, and passed on, and gone down to Gilgal."*

Saul, the king that Israel desired and chose to reign over them instead of God, grieved the heart of God. In short, Saul never followed YeHoVaH, nor obey God's commandments.

However, after Saul's first time of disobedience, Samuel confronts Saul with his sin.

---

[58] It would be a direct descendant of King Agag who orchestrated a scheme to destroy every Jew in the kingdom of Ahasuerus.
[59] Hebrew word 5162. Although interpreted repented here can also be interpreted as sorrowed.

*1 Samuel 15:18-21*

*"And YeHoVaH sent you on a journey, and said, Go and utterly destroy the sinners the Amalekites, and fight against them until they be consumed. Wherefore then did you not obey the voice of YeHoVaH, but did fly upon the spoil, and did evil in the sight of YeHoVaH? And Saul said unto Samuel, Yea, I have obeyed the voice of YeHoVaH, and have gone the way which YeHoVaH sent me, and have brought Agag the king of Amalek, and have utterly destroyed the Amalekites. But the people took of the spoil, sheep and oxen, the chief of the things which should have been utterly destroyed, to sacrifice unto YeHoVaH your God in Gilgal"*

In this passage, we get a glimpse into Saul's thinking.

Saul relates that he indeed obeyed God, leaving out the fact that he left the king of the Amalekites alive. Regarding the spoil, he saw no harm in the people's actions to keep the sheep. After all, their hearts had good intentions: *they were going to use the best of them to offer a sacrifice to YeHoVaH.*

Saul's reasons, however, could not persuade Samuel to change his mind and see things his way. Instead, Samuel relates to Saul the bottom line required to obey God and the reaction of God to Saul's disobedience. .

## Chapter 5:
### A Deceptive Devotion

> 1 Samuel 15:22-23
> 
> And Samuel said, Has YeHoVaH [as great] delight in burnt offerings and sacrifices, as in obeying the voice of YeHoVaH? Behold, to obey [is] better than sacrifice, [and] to listen than the fat of rams. For rebellion [is as] the sin of witchcraft, and stubbornness [is as] iniquity and idolatry. Because you have rejected the word of YeHoVaH, he has also rejected you from [being] king."

Samuel knew the truth about the matter. Saul's rational of the situation did not cut it with Samuel. Even though Saul said he repented, his actions proved otherwise.

> 1 Samuel 15:24-26
> 
> "And Saul said unto Samuel, I have sinned: for I have transgressed the commandment of YeHoVaH, and your words: because I feared the people, and obeyed their voice. Now therefore, I pray you, pardon my sin, and turn again with me, that I may worship YeHoVaH. And Samuel said unto Saul, I will not return with you: for you have rejected the word of YeHoVaH, and YeHoVaH has rejected you from being king over Israel."

Saul's life went on; however, the Spirit of YeHoVaH left him, and an evil spirit plagued him. As Saul's life continued, he became so desperate that he sought a witch to give him the advice he needed before a certain battle. That battle proved to be the last battle Saul would fight, for Saul died in that battle. As the door closes on Saul's life, we find this giant of a man in whom Israel put their trust, fallen and defeated in battle. Hopes of him leading Israel to victory as a nation faded early in his kingship and ended in disaster on the slopes of Mt. Gilboa[60].

Saul's reign as king and his life stands out as a powerful example of one who puts God's commands on the backburner. It shows what happens when one only completes that which satisfies their own heart's goals. Many years later, Jeremiah, the prophet, declared the dangers of following one's own heart:

*Jeremiah 17:9*
*"The heart is deceitful above all things, and desperately wicked: who can know it?"*

Picking up on the theme of a wicked heart, Yeshua taught His disciples to watch what comes from the heart:

*Mark 7:20-23*
*"And he said, That which comes out of the man, that defiles the man. For from within, out of the heart of men, proceed evil thoughts, adulteries, fornications, murders, Thefts, covetousness, wickedness, deceit, lasciviousness, an evil eye, blasphemy, pride,*

---

[60] *1 Samuel 31:1-8*

Chapter 5:
A Deceptive Devotion

*foolishness: All these evil things come from within, and defile the man."*

To avoid deception, one must monitor their heart, discern what matters it holds as supreme. King Saul's life, as well as that of the people who coveted a king of earth over the King of Heaven, present an excellent lesson in the realm of deception.

**Deception promises one thing but delivers another!**

King Saul and the people at that time longed for something they thought would satisfy their need, in this case, a powerful king of earth who would fight battles for them. In their minds, a strong and valiant king would give them the life they desired. Scripture bears witness to that fact in the comment that God told Samuel to relate to the people:

*1 Samuel 8:11 a*
*"And he said, This will be the manner of the king that shall reign over you:"*[61]

---

[61] Remember the details were outlined earlier in this chapter showing what things the king would demand of them.

Unfortunately, these people did not have the foresight to recognize the true realties of what they desired, and when told, they did not want to hear it. They surmised what things would be like for them. They thought they knew better. Their actions made it clear that they did not want God to decide for them. They wanted their own way and to their detriment, they received it.

These people followed a deceptive heart and learned the hard way that deception veils the mind and clouds the truth. It draws the heart to long for a thing which seems important, yet deception has no intentions of presenting it to them.

Here in this chapter, we see deception buffooned a people tired of the repetition of problems and with leaders ruling over them that were not kings. Deception pulled on their dissatisfaction of living within the need of constant deliverance and forwarded another solution. Deception pulled on their desire for a better life and presented that life as fulfilled through a powerful king who would rule and keep the enemies of Israel at bay. Deception led them to follow their dream, using a formula, a solution that rejected God. That solution God never designed.

Regrettably, their heart caused them to reach for a solution of earth and not one from heaven. God promised them peace and a good life if they would be

## Chapter 5:
## A Deceptive Devotion

faithful to Him. Unfortunately, they failed to recognize and embrace God's merciful requirements:

*Deuteronomy 11:22-25*
*"For if you shall diligently keep all these commandments which I command you, to do them, to love YeHoVaH your God, to walk in all his ways, and to cleave unto him; Then will YeHoVaH drive out all these nations from before you, and you shall possess greater nations and mightier than yourselves. Every place where the soles of your feet shall tread shall be yours: from the wilderness and Lebanon, from the river, the river Euphrates, even unto the uttermost sea shall your coast be. There shall no man be able to stand before you: [for] YeHoVaH your God shall lay the fear of you and the dread of you upon all the land that you shall tread upon, as he has said unto you."*

God gave Israel a clear pattern for success. It lay within the parameters of their devotion and service to *Him as their only God*. If deception's snare had not caught Israel; if she had not been deceived but rather followed His advice and received God as their King, they would certainly have found Him more than enough.

Additionally, they would have discovered that their obedience to Him and His laws would have produced the good life for which they longed. Turning away from Him, holding the principles of other nations such as longing for a powerful king, only took Israel on a road to disappointment. This was one more wound from deception's snare.

We know as we study these things that deception cares not for its victims. In fact, it prefers to throw its dark veil over hearts to lead them away from the truth and a rightful devotion to God. It presents the ideals and aspirations of humankind as the superior goal in this life. The bite of deception's snare is hard and cruel, yet it hides its devouring jaws beneath a presentation that seems sweet and gentle. However, deception has no power over those who seek God to know the truth and do things God's way.

> Psalm 19:7-11
> "The law (torah) of YeHoVaH [is] perfect, converting the soul: the testimony of YeHoVaH [is] sure, making wise the simple. The statutes of YeHoVaH [are] right, rejoicing the heart: the commandment of YeHoVaH [is] pure, enlightening the eyes. The fear of YeHoVaH [is] clean, enduring for ever: the judgments of YeHoVaH [are] true [and] righteous altogether. More to be desired [are they] than gold, yea, than much fine gold: sweeter also than honey and the honeycomb. Moreover, by them is your servant warned: [and] in keeping of them [there is] great reward."

**Let us sell out to God and to God alone. In that way we will hold an appropriate dedication and thus, escape a deceptive devotion.**

*A Sinister Snare*

*"Take heed to thyself, lest you make a covenant with the inhabitants of the land whither you go, lest it be for a snare in the midst of you:"*

*Exodus 34:12*

**K**ING SOLOMON, ACCLAIMED during his days as the wisest man in the world, made a very serious mistake. Early in his reign, in his personal life, he committed a grave error which happened for political reasons. By committing this act, Solomon fell into a trap through which none of his wisdom rescued him.

*1 Kings 3:1-3*

*"And Solomon made affinity with Pharaoh king of Egypt, and took Pharaoh's daughter, and brought her into the city of David, until he had made an end of building his own house, and the house of YeHoVaH, and the wall of Jerusalem round about. Only the people sacrificed in high places because there was no house built unto the name of YeHoVaH, until those days. And*

*Solomon loved the YeHoVaH, walking in the statutes of David his father: only he sacrificed and burnt incense in high places."*

In this passage we see that Solomon made affinity, or a covenant agreement with Pharoah, king of Egypt. Such political agreements were commonplace for other nations, but not for Israel. Additionally, Solomon took Pharoah's daughter as his wife as part of that covenant agreement. Additionally, he made a special place for his first wife to worship her Egyptian gods[62].

This error proved fatal to Solomon, for we read in his latter days, he went after other gods.

1 Kings 11:4-8
*"For it came to pass, when Solomon was old, [that] his wives turned away his heart after other gods: and his heart was not perfect with YeHoVaH his God, as [was] the heart of David his father. For Solomon went after Ashtoreth the goddess of the Zidonians, and after Milcom the abomination of the Ammonites. And Solomon did evil in the sight of YeHoVaH, and went not fully after YeHoVaH, as [did] David his father. Then did Solomon build an high place for Chemosh, the abomination of Moab, in the hill that [is] before*

---

[62] Later, as Solomon married other women, he made room for their gods also.

## Chapter 6:
## A Sinister Snare

*Jerusalem, and for Molech, the abomination of the children of Ammon. And likewise did he for all his strange wives, which burnt incense and sacrificed unto their gods."*

With this scripture passage, we see that Solomon never recovered from the snare set for him within that political covenant agreement with Pharoah and his daughter. The Bible makes it clear, Solomon remained snared, as in the end, his wives turned away his heart from YeHoVaH and set it to follow other gods. Solomon never kept his heart guarded or protected as did his father David. While the Bible says Solomon loved YeHoVaH, his heart was not "perfect" with his God.

*1 Kings 11:4 b*
*and his heart was not perfect <8003> with YeHoVaH his God, as [was] the heart of David his father.*

As we look at the word "perfect" <8003>, שָׁלֵם in Hebrew, *pronounced Shalem*, we see it is close to the word שָׁלוֹם, *pronounced Shalom*. In a sense, the two Hebrew words are similar in that *shalem and shalom* indicate *a peace, shalem* implying peace *in the sense of nothing missing*. In that sense, shalem means complete, in the sense of *keeping covenant*[63]. To understand this gives us the root of Solomon's problem. He did not

---

[63] Strong's exhaustive concordance # 8003.

keep his side of the covenant with the God of Israel. In other words, Solomon failed to yield to God and His ways, giving them the full priority they required. In his heart, he held other things of greater value. Therefore, his heart never attained *a oneness with God, a peace with God with nothing missing.*

Later in his life, that heart disloyalty fully manifested as Solomon went after Ashtoreth, the goddess of the Zidonians, and after Milcom the abomination of the Ammonites. Scripture clearly states the reason: ***"his wives turned away his heart after other gods**[64]**."*** As scripture summarizes Solomon's life, it tells us that he did evil in the sight of YeHoVaH and ***went not fully after YeHoVaH as did David his father.***

During Solomon's life, eventually, he built high places to Chemosh, the abomination of Moab, and to Molech, the abomination of the children of Ammon. He also built high places for all his strange wives, to which he burned incense and sacrificed to their gods.

How did YeHoVaH respond to Solomon?

> *1 Kings 11:9-10*
> *"And YeHoVaH was angry with Solomon, because his heart was turned from YeHoVaH God of Israel, which had appeared unto him twice, And had commanded him*

---

[64] *1 Kings 11:4*

## Chapter 6:
## A Sinister Snare

> *concerning this thing, that he should not go after other gods: but he kept not that which YeHoVaH commanded."*

God's anger kindled against Solomon because his heart turned away from YeHoVaH, Who appeared twice to Solomon. We hear of the first appearance to Solomon in 1 Kings 3:5. At that time YeHoVaH asked Solomon a question: "Ask what shall I give you?"

> *1 Kings 3:7-9*
> *"And now, O YeHoVaH my God, you have made your servant king instead of David my father: and I [am but] a little child: I know not [how] to go out or come in. And your servant [is] in the midst of your people which you have chosen, a great people, that cannot be numbered nor counted for multitude. Give therefore your servant an understanding heart to judge your people, that I may discern between good and bad: for who is able to judge this your so great a people?"*

At that time, the heart of Solomon was still tender towards YeHoVaH, and he saw himself as a child in God's eyes, not knowing how to go out or come in. Looking at the great number of people over which Solomon reigned, he asked God for an understanding heart so he could properly judge the people, discerning between good and bad.

God responds favourably to Solomon, granting his request along with riches and honour, even though Solomon did not ask for them. Additionally, God gives Solomon a warning.

> 1 Kings 3:12-14
> *"Behold, I have done according to your words: lo, I have given you a wise and an understanding heart; so that there was none like you before you, neither after you shall any arise like unto you. And I have also given you that which you have not asked, both riches, and honour: so that there shall not be any among the kings like unto you all your days. And if you will walk in my ways, to keep my statutes and my commandments, as your father David did walk, then I will lengthen your days."*

*"If you walk in my ways, to keep my statutes and commandments, as your father David did walk, then I will lengthen your days."* While these words might not seem like a warning, yet their presence indicates something powerful for Solomon to consider: *"if you walk in my ways, to keep my commandments"*. These words should have caused Solomon to inquire about his present behaviour, as well as consider his future path. Yet, immediately after that appearance Solomon made a covenant with Pharoah. Unfortunately, it looks as if Solomon missed the warning.

Yet, God gave him another.

## Chapter 6:
## A Sinister Snare

1 Kings 9:2-9

"That YeHoVaH appeared to Solomon the second time, as he had appeared unto him at Gibeon. And YeHoVaH said unto him, I have heard your prayer and your supplication, that you have made before me: I have hallowed this house, which you have built, to put my name there for ever; and my eyes and my heart shall be there perpetually. **And if you will walk before me, as David your father walked, in integrity of heart, and in uprightness, to do according to all that I have commanded you, [and] will keep my statutes and my judgments: Then I will establish the throne of your kingdom upon Israel for ever, as I promised to David your father, saying, There shall not fail you a man upon the throne of Israel.** "

"[But] if you shall at all turn from following me, you or your children, and will not keep my commandments [and] my statutes which I have set before you, but go and serve other gods, and worship them: Then will I cut off Israel out of the land which I have given them; and this house, which I have hallowed for my name, will I cast out of my sight; and Israel shall be a proverb and a byword among all people: And at this house, [which] is high, every one that passes by it shall be astonished, and shall hiss; and they shall say, Why has YeHoVaH done thus unto this land, and to this house? And they shall answer, Because they forsook YeHoVaH their God, who brought forth their fathers out of the land of Egypt, and *have taken hold upon other gods, and have worshipped them, and served them: therefore has YeHoVaH brought upon them all this evil."*

Here, the warning becomes more emphatic and contains greater detail. However, Solomon failed to heed the warnings of God. While his God-given wisdom to rule faired him well, he failed to apply wisdom to his life beyond the throne. In the end, his choices pushed God right out of his heart. We see this in the word scripture uses when describing Solomon's latter life:

1 Kings 11:9
"*And YeHoVaH was angry with Solomon, because his heart was **turned <5186>** from YeHoVaH God of Israel, which had appeared unto him twice,*"

| Strong's # | Hebrew word turned | Pronunciation |
|---|---|---|
| 5186 | נָטָה | natah<br>naw-taw' |
| Among its meanings are the words to turn aside, pervert or carry aside, or push out of the way. |||

In summary, Solomon allowed his heart to become twisted and turned him away from serving YeHoVaH.

## Chapter 6:
## A Sinister Snare

Let's visit the scripture in 1 Kings 11 again:

> *1 Kings 11:11-12*
> *"And had commanded him concerning this thing, that he should not go after other gods: but he kept not that which YeHoVaH commanded. Wherefore YeHoVaH said unto Solomon, Forasmuch as this is done of you, and you have not kept my covenant and my statutes, which I have commanded you, I will surely rend the kingdom from you and will give it to your servant."*

In this sad tale of Solomon's life, we see the bottom line of his problem: **He kept not that which YeHoVaH commanded.** As Solomon made a covenant with Pharaoh and took Pharaoh's daughter to be his wife, he transgressed his covenant with God and slowly deception began to spin its web.

> *Exodus 34:12*
> *"Take heed to thyself, lest you make a covenant with the inhabitants of the land whither you go, lest it be for a snare in the midst of you:"*

While Solomon made a special place for his Egyptian wife to live along with her gods[65], *(and later for his other wives and their gods)*, the separation he drew with physical distance made no difference. It was an external fix ineffective against an internal problem. It

---

[65] *1 Kings 7:8*

proved inadequate to remove the snare deeply intertwined in his life.

As time went by, slowly but surely, the bait in the snare continued to trap Solomon. His wives' idolatry, while practiced outside of his living space, nevertheless spread like a canker worm. King Solomon, still snared by idolatry's bait, never acknowledged the snare which snagged him. Eventually, as scripture shows us, Solomon worshipped false gods, doing evil in the sight of YeHoVaH.

In the end, unfortunately, Solomon's sin not only affected his own life but, as he was king of Israel, it affected the entire Kingdom. In Israel, especially on the hills surrounding God's city of Jerusalem, idolatry gained a stronghold. Its call led many of Israel's people into the trap of idolatry.

Solomon's divided loyalty saw His kingdom divided. It happened just as YeHoVaH promised if Solomon was unfaithful to Him.

**How could a man, with so much promise, love for God and wisdom, allow his heart to turn away?**

While the answer might seem difficult to grasp, we can give thanks to YeHoVaH for *the insight from His Word*:

## Chapter 6:
## A Sinister Snare

*1 Kings 11:1-4*
*"But king Solomon loved many strange women, together with the daughter of Pharaoh, women of the Moabites, Ammonites, Edomites, Zidonians, [and] Hittites; Of the nations [concerning] which YeHoVaH said unto the children of Israel, You shall not go in to them, neither shall they come in unto you: [for] surely they will turn away your heart after their gods:* **Solomon clave unto these in love.** *And he had seven hundred wives, princesses, and three hundred concubines:* **and his wives turned away his heart.** *For it came to pass, when Solomon was old, [that] his wives turned away his heart after other gods: and his heart was not perfect with YeHoVaH his God, as [was] the heart of David his father.")*

Solomon clave or clung to these in love and his wives turned away (perverted, carried aside) his heart. This shows idolatry's deceptive tactics at work as Solomon put other things before YeHoVaH, as this is the bottom line to idolatry.

When idolatry happens in a life, it matters not the specific tool or source used, but rather one must recognize the violation of the principal warning from scripture. Idolatry[66], as scripture shares, ensnares its

---
[66] Engraved images and statues are only some forms of idolatry. It is better defined as anything which takes the place of God.

victims. In modern terms, idolatry happens like the frog in the pot analogy. Put a frog in a pot of hot water and immediately, it jumps out. Put a frog in warm, comfortable water, it remains. Then, one slowly turns up the heat until it is cooked.

Likewise, Solomon, *in the beginning,* did not prostrate himself before statues of gold or silver. He focused on other things, including how to please his wives. Slowly, the snare enlarged its grip in the secret places of his heart. Quietly, subtly, without noise, the strings of iniquity's web sent out its tentacles. Unfortunately, Solomon recognized it not and so it kept spinning its web in the background.

Never do we hear from Solomon's lips the prayer of King David after he sinned with Bathsheba.

> *Psalm 139:23-24*
> *"Search me, O God, and know my heart: try me, and know my thoughts: And see if there be any wicked way in me, and lead me in the way everlasting."*

At that time, Nathan, the prophet, confronted David. David, immediately recognized his sin, acknowledged it and then repented. David so desired to please God that he wanted every part of his being to love and serve YeHoVaH. He desired God to examine his very thoughts, that which precedes his actions. He understood the removal of any wicked way, would lead to the way everlasting.

Unfortunately, when God called a prophet to declare divine judgment on Solomon, Solomon repented not. Rather, after he heard the prophecy where God would divide the kingdom after his death and appoint a man named Jeroboam to rule over 10 tribes, Solomon sought to kill Jeroboam[67]. Here we see one more perverted avenue of Solomon's heart. Reacting in that manner indicated a contrary heart to that of his father, David.

Truly, Solomon's life shows us that a person's heart, with its deepest thoughts and desires, becomes ensnared when other things come before God. It is best for every person to expose their heart to the only light which reveals it all, the Light of Yeshua. Then, as He reveals the depths of our heart to us, we have opportunity to humbly receive His rebuke.

To learn a lesson from Solomon, let us remember to guard our hearts and continually ask our loving heavenly Father to search us. In doing so, we trust that He reveal to us our ways which are contrary to His ways. By doing this, we set ourselves up to face God's

---

[67] *1 Kings 11:3-40*

realities and hopefully, escape all sinister snares and instead, walk as one with Him.

Oh God, may we truly have eyes to see, ears to hear, and a heart to perceive what Your Spirit says. May You impart whatever we need to come before You to seek Your face. As you speak to us, may the Holy Spirit give us wisdom to recognize even the smallest thread or tendency drawing us away from You. Through our repentance, may we see every offensive thing to You mercifully removed from our lives.

*Dear God, with Your help, and through the power of the Holy Spirit, help us to recognize, identify and root out every sinister snare ha satan sends (or has sent) our way.*

# COURSE 602

# 7

### A Corrupted Counsel

*"For they are a nation void of counsel, neither is there any understanding in them. O that they were wise, that they understood this, that they would consider their latter end! How should one chase a thousand, and two put ten thousand to flight, except their Rock had sold them, and YeHoVaH had shut them up?"*

Deuteronomy 32:28-30

**J**EROBOAM BECAME NORTHERN ISRAEL'S first king. He was God's choice to rule. Earlier, through the words of Ahijah, the prophet, God promised Jeroboam this rule along with a magnificent kingdom and a powerful legacy.

1 Kings 11:29-36

> *"And it came to pass at that time when Jeroboam went out of Jerusalem, that the prophet Ahijah the Shilonite found him in the way; and he had clad himself with a new garment; and they two were alone in the field: And Ahijah caught the new garment that was on him, and rent it in twelve pieces: And he said to Jeroboam, Take*

*ten pieces: for thus said YeHoVaH, the God of Israel, Behold, I will rend the kingdom out of the hand of Solomon, and will give ten tribes to you: (But he shall have one tribe for my servant David's sake, and for Jerusalem's sake, the city which I have chosen out of all the tribes of Israel:) Because that they have forsaken me, and have worshipped Ashtoreth the goddess of the Zidonians, Chemosh the god of the Moabites, and Milcom the god of the children of Ammon, and have not walked in my ways, to do that which is right in my eyes, and to keep my statutes and my judgments, as did David his father. However I will not take the whole kingdom out of his hand: but I will make him prince all the days of his life for David my servant's sake, whom I chose, because he kept my commandments and my statutes: But I will take the kingdom out of his son's hand, and will give it unto you, even ten tribes. And unto his son will I give one tribe, that David my servant may have a light alway before me in Jerusalem, the city which I have chosen me to put my name there."*

Recapping the deliverance of this word, we see it came through a prophetic act. Ahijah, the prophet, donned a new tallit[68]. Tallits, among other things in scripture

---

[68] King James says, "new garment", however, Jewish scholars tell us it was a tallit. A tallit is a prayer mantle with much prophetic symbolism.

## Chapter 7
## A Corrupted Counsel

can represent the Kingdom of God[69]. Ahijah, following his assignment from God, sought out Jeroboam. He found him in a field and there, delivered to him the word of God. Jeroboam, a man who Solomon made a leader over the tribe of Joseph, (the ten tribes of Israel in the North[70]) standing in a field on that day, witnessed a prophetic act which demonstrated God's plan to divide the kingdom of Israel.

As Jeroboam watched, Ahijah took the new tallit from off his shoulders. Then, with Jeroboam watching, he tore it into twelve pieces. Ahijah gave Jeroboam ten pieces[71]. As he did, he said to him what we read earlier:

### *1 Kings 11:31-32*
*"Take ten pieces: for thus said YeHoVaH, the God of Israel, Behold, I will rend (tear) the kingdom out of the hand of Solomon, and will give ten tribes to you: (But*

---

[69] In *1 Samuel 15:27-28* we see Saul tearing Samuel's tallit, at which point Samuel uses Saul's actions as confirmation that God would rend the kingdom from Saul's hand. *"And as Samuel turned about to go away, he laid hold upon the skirt of his mantle, and it rent. And Samuel said unto him, The LORD has rent the kingdom of Israel from you this day, and has given it to a neighbour of you, that is better than you."*

[70] *1 Kings 11:28* *"And the man Jeroboam [was] a mighty man of valour: and Solomon seeing the young man that he was industrious, he made him ruler over all the charge of the house of Joseph."*

[71] *1 Kings 11:30-31*

> he (Solomon) shall have one tribe for my servant David's sake, and for Jerusalem's sake, the city which I have chosen out of all the tribes of Israel:)."

Then Ahijah added:

> 1 Kings 11:37-38
> "And I will take you, and you shall reign according to all that your soul desires and shall be king over Israel. And it shall be, if you will listen unto all that I command you, and will walk in my ways, and do that is right in my sight, to keep my statutes and my commandments, as David my servant did; that I will be with you and build you a sure house, as I built for David, and will give Israel unto you."

Here's the crux of the matter in the prophetic act Ahijah did for Jeroboam. God would tear apart the kingdom of Israel. Ten tribes of Israel[72] God would hand over to Jeroboam to reign over as King[73]. If Jeroboam followed God's commandments and walked in His ways doing that which was right in God's eyes as King David did, then Jeroboam's reward would be as dynamic as that of King David, including an enduring lineage.

---

[72] The rest of the tribes would remain with Solmon's son.
[73] Remember, earlier Solomon set Jeroboam over the same 10 tribes.

## Chapter 7
## A Corrupted Counsel

Just as God gave David seed to sit on the throne, so God would do for Jeroboam.

Earlier in the prophecy, God explained why He would divide the kingdom. God made it clear that His Divine actions came because of Israel's actions. Israel worshipped false gods, the names of which Ahijah specifically listed. He added, also, comments regarding Israel's present failure to walk in God's ways, His statutes and judgments. He emphasized their inability to please God and do that which was right in God's eyes.

In other words, YeHoVaH explained to Jeroboam, through his unforgettable encounter with Ahijah, the bottom-line of the behaviour directly responsible for God's actions to make Israel a divided kingdom.

> *1 Kings 11:33*
> *Because that they have forsaken me, and have worshipped Ashtoreth the goddess of the Zidonians, Chemosh the god of the Moabites, and Milcom the god of the children of Ammon, and have not walked in my ways, to do [that which is] right in my eyes, and [to keep] my statutes and my judgments, as [did] David his father.*

With Jeroboam given all these details, he walked away from that encounter with the prophet, Ahijah, armed with ample knowledge to keep the entrusted part of the kingdom in the north aligned with God. In addition, he had enough information to allow it to fail by worshipping false gods, just as Israel did during the reign of Solomon.

To put it another way, Jeroboam knew:
- **To keep the kingdom entrusted to him**, he must keep God's commandments and statutes, walk in God's ways, doing that which was right in God's eyes.
- **To lose the kingdom entrusted to him,** forsake God's commandments and statutes, do not walk in God's ways, nor do that which was right in God's eyes.

Following this encounter with God's true prophet, Jeroboam needed to flee for his life. Solomon's receptivity of the same prophetic word aroused him to anger. He then issued a death decree for Jeroboam. Jeroboam fled to Egypt until after King Solomon's death.

## KING JEROBOAM COMES TO THE THRONE
The ten tribes of Joseph never stood alone as a nation before. While a murmuring existed between the ten tribes in the north and the other two in the south, they united to live as one under King David. After his death when Solomon took the throne, a rift began to

## Chapter 7
## A Corrupted Counsel

manifest. Additionally, Solomon increased taxes to pay for his many building projects, much to the discontent of the people. Nearing the end of Solomon's reign, the people found the tax burden too heavy to bear[74].

After Solomon's death when Rehoboam sat on David's throne, emissaries came to him to plead for lesser taxes. Rehoboam consulted with his counsellors, both old and young, but received conflicting advice. From the older, more experienced men, Rehoboam heard instructions to serve the people and thereby lessen the tax burden. Rehoboam's younger, inexperienced counsellors cared not for the servant like attitude but rather took a dictatorial stance. They advised Solomon to show his strength by promising to implement even greater taxes. Rehoboam decided to go with the counsel of his younger companions and expressed that decision to the gathered tribal leaders[75].

This decision reverberated hard throughout the kingdom, shaking it like an earthquake. Tribes in the north, (the ten tribes of Joseph), refused to serve king Rehoboam and openly rejected him. Then, they called for Jeroboam and made him King over them.

---

[74] *1 Kings 12:4*
[75] *1 Kings 12:6-14*

DECEIVED.
How Errors in a Faith System Affect Both God & His People.

*1 Kings 12:16-20*
*"So when all Israel saw that the king hearkened not unto them, the people answered the king, saying, What portion have we in David? neither [have we] inheritance in the son of Jesse: to your tents, O Israel: now see to you own house, David. So Israel departed unto their tents. But [as for] the children of Israel which dwelt in the cities of Judah, Rehoboam reigned over them. Then king Rehoboam sent Adoram, who [was] over the tribute; and all Israel stoned him with stones, that he died. Therefore, king Rehoboam made speed to get him up to his chariot, to flee to Jerusalem. So Israel rebelled against the house of David unto this day. And it came to pass, when all Israel heard that Jeroboam was come again, that they sent and called him unto the congregation, and made him king over all Israel: there was none that followed the house of David, but the tribe of Judah only."*

Rehoboam reacted strongly to the actions of the ten tribes, especially to the making of Jeroboam their king. As a result, a civil war promised to erupt in Israel. However, God intervened. Through the mouth of a prophet to Rehoboam, God stated this division came from His direct hand.

*1 Kings 12:22-24*
*"But the word of God came unto Shemaiah the man of God, saying, Speak unto Rehoboam, the son of Solomon,*

## Chapter 7
## A Corrupted Counsel

*king of Judah, and unto all the house of Judah and Benjamin, and to the remnant of the people, saying, Thus said YeHoVaH, You shall not go up, nor fight against your brethren the children of Israel: return every man to his house; for this thing is from me. They listened therefore to the word of YeHoVaH, and returned to depart, according to the word of YeHoVaH."*

Thus began the divided kingdom with Israel in the north and Judah, the Levites and the tribe of Benjamin in the south.

**JEROBOAM AND THE NORTHERN KINGDOM**
After his installation as king[76], Jeroboam attempted to establish his kingdom. He made Shechem his royal city and began to do some minor building projects. However, early in his reign, Jeroboam feared losing the tribes that currently followed him. To counteract that fear and to keep his kingdom, Jeroboam consulted with his appointed counsellors. Then Jeroboam made a tragic decision which set Northern Israel on a course against YeHoVaH.

Jeroboam changed his kingdom's worship system. He kept the name of YeHoVaH as Israel's God but made a house of high places and ordained a feast along the lines of the feast of tabernacles but with added

---

[76] *1 Kings 12:20*

components. He set up two golden calves, one in Dan *(further north)* and one Bethel *(closer to Jerusalem[77])*, saying to Israel, these are the gods O Israel that brought you out of Egypt[78]. Additionally, Jeroboam made priests of the lowest people, not sons of Levi[79]. These priests knew not the laws of God, nor His commandments, nor His ways. In short, Jeroboam exchanged the invisible God of Abraham, Isaac and Jacob for visible golden calves, set up a parallel system of worship to that which God ordained, altering it in places to meet his needs.

Did Jeroboam remember the warning from Ahijah regarding foreign gods? Possibly. Jeroboam did not use any of the gods Ahijah mentioned, however, Jeroboam missed the point on idolatry altogether. He overlooked the most important aspect of the true God's faith system: *to do that which is right in the eyes of the living God, YeHoVaH.* Instead, Jeroboam manipulated the people with lies and adjusted the true faith to accommodate his fears. Jeroboam's life, a great disappointment to God, ended with a declaration of God's dissatisfaction as well as a decree to end the line of Jeroboam[80].

---

[77] Bethel is about 12 miles or so North of Jerusalem.
[78] *1 Kings 12:28*
[79] *1 Kings 12:26-32*
[80] At one point in his reign when his son was ill, he sent his wife to Ahijah incognito for a word from YeHoVaH. *1 Kings 14::7-16*

## Chapter 7
## A Corrupted Counsel

**JEROBOAM'S WEAKNESS**

Jeroboam failed to grasp the importance of serving YeHoVaH *in a manner that pleased Him*. He did not use wisdom in his service to God, even though he knew that Solomon and Israel failed God because they gave themselves over to idolatry. Yet Jeroboam did the same thing.

> *1 Kings 12:26-27*
> *"And Jeroboam said in his heart, Now shall the kingdom return to the house of David: If this people go up to do sacrifice in the house of YeHoVaH at Jerusalem, then shall the heart of this people turn again unto their lord, even unto Rehoboam king of Judah, and they shall kill me, and go again to Rehoboam king of Judah."*

When Jeroboam sought counsellors for himself, he went not to God's ordained sources such as a prophet like Ahijah. In fact, Ahijah was alive[81] but rather than reach out to a true prophet of God for Godly counsel, Jeroboam invented a new worship system for Northern Israel using golden calves. Putting one near Jerusalem was an obvious scheme to keep the lower half of his kingdom from going to Jerusalem. Erecting another calf a lot further north would accommodate the most northern tribes.

---

[81] *1 Kings 14:2-4*

Jeroboam, as his actions reveal, did not have a relationship with YeHoVaH as David did. Additionally, he thought it not wrong to present to the people a faith system, which had similarities to the truth, but perverted the faith at its deepest point. He substituted other gods and modified ordained feasts to suit his need. In other words, Jeroboam presented to Northern Israel a parallel but perverted faith system.

## A SIMILAR SYSTEM

Have you heard it said, "History repeats itself." Indeed, it does. Jeroboam's error Constantine the great imitated. He married Christianity to the many gods of Greek worship. He introduced worship of the saints, adjusted the feasts and other days of worship, as well as introduced other pagan practices into Christianity forbidden by scripture.

Today, many people recognize Constantine's additions yet abandoning them seems extremely difficult. When presenting truth regarding their practices in the hopes of exposing error, many say, "well, that is not what it means to me". In these cases, it seems apparent that deception still masks some minds to the realities of scripture.

## Chapter 7
## A Corrupted Counsel

**Once again, the bottom line of a pure and holy faith system is believers doing what is right in God's own eyes, and not their own eyes.**

Deception robs of good counsel. Deception removes understanding and eradicates wisdom. Deception's goal positions people to live a life of defeat. Remember this scripture?

> *Deuteronomy 32:28-30*
> *"For they are a nation void of counsel, neither is there any understanding in them. O that they were wise, that they understood this, that they would consider their latter end! How should one chase a thousand, and two put ten thousand to flight, except their Rock had sold them, and YeHoVaH had shut them up?"*

## DECEPTION'S ANTIDOTE

It is time that we expose deception's tactics. It is time that we give deception a kick even if it means weighing out in the scriptures every aspect of our faith to ensure its accuracy. To overcome any form of deception, we must trust God's counsel and weigh out what we believe and why against those counsels.

In other words, believers must learn the scriptures and their meaning for themselves, even if it means looking *to the original transcripts* wherever possible to hear exactly the way in which God wrote the scriptures. This helps us to determine exactly what He desires for us and from us. These may seem difficult words, but deception is a cruel and vicious foe. While we have compassion on its victims, we must give deception no room to operate! We must learn to weigh all things out as scripture dictates, *pleasing the God of the Bible, giving Him what He requires.*

After all, it is by His standards and through His specified door that we enter the kingdom.

> John 10:7-14
> *"Then said Jesus unto them again, Verily, verily, I say unto you, I am the door of the sheep. All that ever came before me are thieves and robbers: but the sheep did not hear them. I am the door: by me if any man enter in, he shall be saved, and shall go in and out, and find pasture. The thief comes not, but for to steal, and to kill, and to destroy: I am come that they might have life, and that they might have [it] more abundantly. I am the good shepherd: the good shepherd gives his life for the sheep. But he that is an hireling, and not the shepherd, whose own the sheep are not, sees the wolf coming, and leaves the sheep, and flees: and the wolf catches them, and scatters the sheep. The hireling flees, because he is an hireling, and cares not for the sheep. I am the good shepherd, and know my [sheep], and am known of mine."*

**Let us seek the direction of the Good Shepherd and totally reject the corrupted counsels of deception.**

# 8

### A Perilous Partnership

*"The hills melted like wax at the presence of YeHoVaH, at the presence of the Lord of the whole earth. The heavens declare his righteousness, and all the people see his glory. Confounded be all they that serve graven images, that boast themselves of idols: worship him, all you gods."*

Psalm 97:5-7

*I*N THE YEAR 874 BCE[82], Ahab, the son of Omri, the sixth king of Northern Israel, came to the throne. His father's legacy carried with it great distain for Omri did greater evil than any king before him[83]. As detrimental as that legacy proved to be, Ahab topped his father's legacy in the evil that he did.

---

[82] In accordance with secular records, Ahab came to the throne 874 BCE (before common era) and reigned 22 years to 853 BCE. wikipedia.org/wiki/Ahab#:~:text=Ahab%20became%20king%20of%20Israel,reign%20to%20871–852%20BC..

[83] 1 Kings 16:25-26 *"But Omri wrought evil in the eyes of YeHoVaH, and did worse than all that [were] before him. For he walked in all the*

## DECEIVED.
### How Errors in a Faith System Affect Both God & His People.

*1 Kings 16:28-30*
*"So Omri slept with his fathers and was buried in Samaria: and Ahab his son reigned in his stead. And in the thirty and eighth year of Asa king of Judah began Ahab the son of Omri to reign over Israel: and Ahab the son of Omri reigned over Israel in Samaria twenty and two years. And Ahab the son of Omri did evil in the sight of YeHoVaH above all that [were] before him."*

Scripture points out the wicked things done by Ahab, including the fact that he brought greater idolatry to Northern Israel than any other king before him. First, he took for his wife, a woman named Jezebel, the daughter King of the Zidonians, who worshipped and served Baal. When Ahab married Jezebel, he became one with her, including worshipping and serving Baal.

*1 Kings 16:31-33*
*"And it came to pass, as if it had been a light thing for him to walk in the sins of Jeroboam the son of Nebat, that he took to wife Jezebel the daughter of Ethbaal king of the Zidonians, and* **went and served Baal, and worshipped him.** *[84]And he reared up an altar for Baal*

---

*way of Jeroboam the son of Nebat, and in his sin wherewith he made Israel to sin, to provoke YeHoVaH God of Israel to anger with their vanities."*

[84] Some research suggests that Ahab served YHVH, however, this scripture presents the truth saying that Ahab went served Baal.

## Chapter 8
## A Perilous Partnership

*in the house of Baal, which he had built in Samaria. And Ahab made a grove; and Ahab did more to provoke YeHoVaH God of Israel to anger than all the kings of Israel that were before him."*

It was the custom in those days for people to worship the same deity as the king. Consequently, as Ahab embraced Jezebel and her gods, so too did most of the people of Israel[85]. Therefore, worship of YeHoVaH declined and worship to Baal increased.

To worship Baal, like the worship to other idols, broke covenant with YeHoVaH and carried with it a penalty.

*Deuteronomy 11:16-17*
*"Take heed to yourselves, that your heart be not deceived, and you turn aside, and serve other gods, and worship them; And [then] YeHoVaH's wrath be kindled against you, and he shut up the heaven, that there be no rain, and that the land yield not her fruit; and [lest] you perish quickly from off the good land which YeHoVaH gave you."*

---

[85] Scripture clearly states that God kept 7,000 who did not bow their knees to Baal or kiss him. *1 Kings 19:18"Yet I have left [me] seven thousand in Israel, all the knees which have not bowed unto Baal, and every mouth which has not kissed him."*

DECEIVED.
How Errors in a Faith System Affect Both God & His People.

As a direct result of the increased idolatry in Israel, YeHoVaH, *just as His Word declared*, sent a drought. This indicated God's displeasure with the broken covenant, but before the drought began, God called a prophet named Elijah to speak with Ahab. Elijah came to Ahab and told him that no rain would fall in Israel until he gave the word. Then Elijah went to a secure, quiet place away from the wrath of the king.

After three years of drought, a water scarcity meant many of the brooks dried up and waters in the rivers lessened. This lack of water caused a food famine in the land as well as the disappearance of grassy meadows to feed the animals. In short, the drought created difficulties for the survival of both humans and beasts.

Now, on one particular day, Ahab, and the governor of his house, Obadiah, went out looking for a grassland so that the royal horses and mules might feed and thus live. To make their search easier, Ahab went in one direction and Obadiah in another.

*1 Kings 18:6-11*
*"So they divided the land between them to pass throughout it: Ahab went one way by himself, and Obadiah went another way by himself. And as Obadiah was in the way, behold, Elijah met him: and he knew him, and fell on his face, and said, [Are] you that my*

## Chapter 8
## A Perilous Partnership

> lord Elijah? And he answered him, I [am]: go, tell your lord, Behold, Elijah [is here]. And he said, What have I sinned, that you would deliver your servant into the hand of Ahab, to slay me? [As] YeHoVaH your God lives, there is no nation or kingdom, whither my lord has not sent to seek you: and when they said, [He is] not [there]; he took an oath of the kingdom and nation, that they found you not. And now you say, Go, tell your lord, Behold, Elijah [is here]."

In this scripture passage, we see that as Obadiah went his way to search for some grasslands, Elijah appears right in front of him. Elijah orders Obadiah to inform Ahab of his whereabouts, however, Obadiah panics. Then, he explains to Elijah that the king has searched high and low for him and is furious since he cannot find him.

### 1 Kings 18:12-14

> "And it shall come to pass, [as soon as] I am gone from you, that the Spirit of YeHoVaH shall carry you whither I know not; and [so] when I come and tell Ahab, and he cannot find you, he shall slay me: but I your servant fear YeHoVaH from my youth. Was it not told my lord what I did when Jezebel slew the prophets of YeHoVaH, how I hid an hundred men of YeHoVaH's

prophets[86] *by fifty in a cave, and fed them with bread and water? And now you say, Go, tell your lord, Behold, Elijah [is here]: and he shall slay me."*

Obadiah recounts the troubling facts of how YeHoVaH suddenly transports Elijah, taking him where no one knew and that would cause a problem for Obadiah, as Ahab would kill him for allowing Elijah to escape. Elijah reassures Obadiah that he will be there when he returns with Ahab.

Obadiah goes to find Ahab. Finding him, they return together so Ahab stands face to face with Elijah. Immediately upon their meeting, Ahab points a finger of blame at Elijah for Israel's trouble.

*1 Kings 18:17*
*"And it came to pass, when Ahab saw Elijah, that Ahab said unto him, [Are] you he that troubleth Israel?"*

Elijah, as the prophet of God, puts the finger of blame where it belonged:

*1 Kings 18:18*
*"And he answered, I have not troubled Israel; but you, and your father's house, in that you and your father[87]*

---

[86] Note here the number of prophets that Obadiah hid. Obviously, Elijah was not the only prophet!
[87] KJV says "you" which is the plural of you, implying you and your father.

## Chapter 8
## A Perilous Partnership

*have forsaken the commandments of YeHoVaH and you have followed Baalim."*

Not only did Elijah put the blame where it belonged, he also reminded Ahab of the reason for the problem, namely, *you and your father's house forsook the commandments of YeHoVaH, and you have followed Baalim".*

Elijah, to cause the people of Northern Israel to repent, introduces a simple contest to prove who was God, either Baal or YeHoVaH. Whichever deity lights the fire of a fresh sacrifice offered to them proves that he is the one true God. Ahab agrees. He follows Elijah's instructions and brings the 450 prophets of Baal as well as 400 prophets who served Baal in the groves[88].

As the contest begins, Baal's priests set up a new sacrifice to Baal and call upon Baal to light the fire. As the day goes on, Baal's servants cry out to him, time after time. They try all their tricks, even cutting themselves in the hopes that Baal would recognize their dedication and thus, hear and answer them. They do this from morning until the time of the evening sacrifice. Elijah taunts them. They keep on trying but could not produce as much as spark.

---

[88] 1 Kings 18:19 *"Now therefore send, and gather to me all Israel unto mount Carmel, and the prophets of Baal four hundred and fifty, and the prophets of the groves four hundred, which eat at Jezebel's table."*

Then, Elijah decides it's time to prove YeHoVaH as the living and true God. He rebuilds the altar of YeHoVaH, has ditches dug around that altar and commands that the sacrifice, the altar stones, and the wood to be dossed with barrels of water. They used so much water that the runoff fills up the ditches around the altar. This action of Elijah eliminates any possibility of spontaneous combustion.

Then, Elijah prays a simple prayer.

> 1 Kings 18:36-39
> "And it came to pass at [the time of] the offering of the [evening] sacrifice[89], that Elijah the prophet came near, and said, YeHoVaH God of Abraham, Isaac, and of Israel, let it be known this day that you [are] God in Israel, and [that] I [am] your servant, and [that] I have done all these things at your word. Hear me, O YeHoVaH, hear me, that this people may know that you [are] YeHoVaH God, and [that] you have turned their heart back again. Then the fire of YeHoVaH fell, and consumed the burnt sacrifice, and the wood, and the stones, and the dust, and licked up the water that [was] in the trench. And when all the people saw [it], they fell on their faces: and they said, YeHoVaH, he [is] the God; YeHoVaH, he [is] the God."

---

[89] Probably 3 p.m. as that was the usual time they offered the evening sacrifice.

## Chapter 8
## A Perilous Partnership

As this encounter closes, Elijah sees to it that all the prophets of Baal meet with their death. Additionally, Elijah gives the word to Ahab that rain is on its way[90] In other words, Ahab, no more drought. With those words, Elijah fulfils the word that he spoke to Ahab three years ago:

> 1 Kings 17:1
> *"And Elijah the Tishbite, who was of the inhabitants of Gilead, said unto Ahab, As YeHoVaH God of Israel liveth, before whom I stand, there shall not be dew nor rain these years, but according to my word."*

## A SPIRITUAL PARALLEL

This entire scenario of the drought which came by Elijah's word, brings to light a spiritual parallel. Water and the result of its absence teach us that:

**Water brings life. Its absence brings death.**

Likewise, worship of the true God brings life, while the worship of false gods brings death. Next, the water symbolizes the Word of God[91], that which the prophet speaks. A prophet whose words come true, and who

---

[90] *1 Kings 18:41*
[91] *Ephesians 5:26 "That he might sanctify and cleanse it with the washing of water by the word,"*

serves the living and true God, proves that YeHoVaH sent that prophet[92].

Spiritually speaking, **God's Word brings life. Its absence brings death.** We see this demonstrated here in the lives of Ahab and Elijah, but also, later in Northern Israel when, near to the end of that kingdom, God spoke of a famine of the word. That word came through the mouth of the prophet, Amos.

> *Amos 8:11*
> *"Behold, the days come, said the Lord YeHoVaH, that I will send a famine in the land, not a famine of bread, nor a thirst for water, but of hearing the words of YeHoVaH:"*

Throughout its 200 plus years of existence, time after time, God confronted the sins of Northern Israel until, finally their refusal to repent brought the death of that kingdom.

Looking back on Ahab in this chapter, we see that as idolatry increased and more people walked away from serving YeHoVaH. That lack of service meant spiritual death. Yet, through it all we see God's mercy for YeHoVaH never forsook the covenant He made with Abraham.

---

[92] *Deuteronomy 18:20-22*

## Chapter 8
## A Perilous Partnership

Moreover, during the time of Ahab, YeHoVaH managed to keep for Himself seven thousand people who never bowed to Baal nor kissed him. As far as YeHoVaH's prophets go, while Elijah conjectured that he was the only prophet left that served YeHoVaH, scripture tells us differently. We hear of situations with Ahab were other prophets of YeHoVaH prophesied to him[93]. All these situations intimate to us the greatness of our God, the depth of His mercy and love. It shows us how much He desires that man repent and return to Him.

> 2 Peter 3:9
> *"The Lord is not slack concerning his promise, as some men count slackness; but is longsuffering to us-ward, not willing that any should perish, but that all should come to repentance."*

### DECEPTION'S DEFLECTION

We gain many lessons from Ahab, Elijah and other participants in this part of the first book of Kings. However, as our study here deals with deception, let us look closer at Ahab's encounter with Elijah, specifically, the meeting at the end of the three-year drought. Remember Ahab's comment to Elijah?

---

[93] *1 Kings 20:13,22,38 1 Kings 22:7*

*1 Kings 18:17*
*"And it came to pass, when Ahab saw Elijah, that Ahab said unto him, [Are] you he that troubleth Israel?"*

Remember Elijah's response?

*1 Kings 18:18*
*"And he answered, I have not troubled Israel; but you, and your father's house, in that you and your father have forsaken the commandments of YeHoVaH and you have followed Baalim."*

Here, we see another important trait of deception. It wants to hide, to keep from being discovered. It, therefore, immediately deflects away from itself, therefore, explaining the finger of blame tactic. In that encounter when Elijah faced Ahab, deception pointed its finger of blame towards Elijah. Elijah, however, put the blame where it belonged and explained what deception tried to hide:

*"You, and your father's house have forsaken the commandments of YeHoVaH and you have followed Baalim"*[94].

---

[94] *1 Kings 18:18 b)*

## Chapter 8
## A Perilous Partnership

Ahab sought Elijah throughout that three-year drought even in nations outside of Northern Israel, **but unfortunately, not for his counsel.** If he had, the drought would have ended much sooner. Instead, deception's accusing mentality entangled Ahab:

> *1 Kings 18:10*
> *"As YeHoVaH your God lives, there is no nation or kingdom, whither my lord has not sent to seek you: and when they said, He is not there; he took an oath of the kingdom and nation, that they found you not."*

Deception, with its deflected blame, stood in the way of Ahab clearly grasping the bottom line of the situation. Without acknowledgment of that truth which deception hid, how could Ahab repent? He could not.

Deception continued in Ahab's life building resentment and hatred for Elijah. As Ahab hunted for Elijah he did so with a passion, willing to kill anyone who would let Elijah escape, hide him or lie to the king regarding his whereabouts. So great was his deception that he even risked wars with nations over the whereabouts of Elijah[95].

---

[95] *1 Kings 18:10*

One of deception's habits, therefore, paints itself and its victims with the brush of *innocence*. Then, it *deflects the blame elsewhere*. In this manner, the root of the problem remains intact. In the case with Elijah and Ahab, deception played its role in deceiving Ahab. That deception with its finger of blame consumed Ahab, becoming an obsession to get hold of Elijah. Of course, God protected Elijah, for He is far greater than deception, its plans and its purposes.

In closing this chapter, we leave Northern Israel with its idolatry in full swing. While Elijah managed to kill the prophets of Baal, Baal worship continued in Northern Israel under the protective eye of Queen Jezebel and her agreeing husband, Ahab.

Eventually, after God sent to no avail numerous prophets to declare the truth and a coming judgment, Northern Israel ended. As it did, its throne ended without even one boast of a *good king* who sat upon it. Every king that sat on that throne, the Bible says, did evil in the sight of YeHoVaH[96]. Eventually, due to the kings' idolatrous behaviour and the nation's refusal to repent, God scattered Northern Israel to the four

---

[96] In places the wording may not be the same, but the meaning is clear that no king in Northern Israel ever did good in the sight of YeHoVaH.

## Chapter 8
## A Perilous Partnership

corners of the earth. However, in mercy, God promised to regather them in their latter years[97]..

May YeHoVaH give us discernment to recognize the disguise and deflection patterns of deception. **May each one of us reject any alliance with deception recognizing that it,** *just like the partnership with Ahab and Jezebel,* **constitutes a perilous partnership, one to completely avoid.**

---

[97] That regathering began in 1948 and continues to this day.

> **Note**
>
> This chapter concludes the major examples of deception which we will study regarding Northern Israel. While other examples exist, time does not permit us to study them in this book. However, as you speak with Holy Spirit and prayerfully read through the book of Kings and Chronicles, you are sure to discover more.
>
> So, we leave Northern Israel behind and focus on Judah.

# 9

*A Deadly Defence*

*"Great is YeHoVaH, and greatly to be praised in the city of our God, in the mountain of his holiness. Beautiful for situation, the joy of the whole earth, is mount Zion, on the sides of the north, the city of the great King."*

Psalm 48:1-2

*A*S WE LEAVE LIFE in Northern Israel behind, we focus on the smaller kingdom in the south. Comprised of the tribe of Judah, it boasted of Jerusalem as its capital. Jerusalem, after the kingdom split, continued to function as it did under King Solomon, only with Rehoboam, Solomon's son, on the throne. Scripture recaps the reign of Rehoboam.

> 1 Kings 14:21-24
> 
> "And Rehoboam the son of Solomon reigned in Judah. Rehoboam [was] forty and one years old when he began to reign, and he reigned seventeen years in Jerusalem,

*the city which YeHoVaH did choose out of all the tribes of Israel, to put his name there. And his mother's name [was] Naamah an Ammonitess.* **And Judah did evil in the sight of YeHoVaH,** *and they provoked him to jealousy with their sins which they had committed, above all that their fathers had done. For they also built them high places, and images, and groves, on every high hill, and under every green tree. And there were also sexual offenders[98] in the land: [and] they did according to all the abominations of the nations which YeHoVaH cast out before the children of Israel."*

This passage clarifies that the course which Judah began under King Solomon continued under Rehoboam. only it became worse. This kingdom added to the worship of YeHoVaH abominations which He abhorred, including the very ones which God earlier commanded Israel to remove from the land of Canaan.

*Leviticus 18:25-30*
*"And the land is defiled: therefore, I do visit the iniquity thereof upon it, and the land itself vomits out her inhabitants. You shall therefore keep my statutes and my judgments, and shall not commit [any] of these*

---

[98] KJV uses the word sodomites, but translators, in believing they understand the intentions, use the term shrine/cult prostitutes, or sexual offenders.

## Chapter 9
## A Deadly Defence

> *abominations; [neither] any of your own nation, nor any stranger that sojourns among you: (For all these abominations have the men of the land done, which [were] before you, and the land is defiled;) That the land spue not you out also, when you defile it, as it spued out the nations that [were] before you. For whosoever shall commit any of these abominations, even the souls that commit [them] shall be cut off from among their people. Therefore shall you keep my ordinance, that [you] commit not [any one] of these abominable customs, which were committed before you, and that you defile not yourselves therein: I [am] YeHoVaH your God."*

Judah's inhabitants, as well as many of those within the temple setting, embraced those abominations which God hated.

Looking back on the situation with eyes from today, one might wonder how such a thing happens. **How can a people given so much, including victory over their enemies from the hand of God, become participants in the very abominations, which God used them to remove.**

While the quick answer points an accurate finger to a form of deception, the longer answer requires a more detailed explanation. Rather than go there, we will use an illustration which God gave to the prophet Ezekiel to explain deception's path to captives of Judah in

Babylon. However, before elaborating on that illustration, we must first look at Israel's once impregnable mindset.

## AN IMPREGNABLE MINDSET

God called Ezekiel, the prophet, to prophesy to the captives the destruction of Jerusalem, including its sacred temple. He, like the prophet in Jerusalem, Jeremiah, encountered an incredible problem. A mindset existed among the Jews of that day, which held to the thought that no one could conquer Jerusalem because the temple of YeHoVaH stood in its midst.

To address this mindset, the prophet Jeremiah outrightly declared the deception:

*Jeremiah 7:1-4*
*"The word that came to Jeremiah from YeHoVaH, saying, Stand in the gate of YeHoVaH's house, and proclaim there this word, and say, Hear the word of YeHoVaH, all you of Judah, that enter in at these gates to worship YeHoVaH. Thus said YeHoVaH of hosts, the God of Israel, Amend your ways and your doings, and I will cause you to dwell in this place. Trust you not in lying words, saying, The temple of YeHoVaH, The temple of YeHoVaH, The temple of YeHoVaH, are these."*

## Chapter 9
## A Deadly Defence

Jeremiah addressed the worshippers coming before the temple of YeHoVaH to worship Him. In the crowd that day, present would be a mixture of faithful servants of God, as well as those who gave Him lip service[99]. Nevertheless, Jeremiah addressed them with a call to repent: *"amend your ways and your doings"*[100]. To that repentance call, Jeremiah adds a promise, *" and I will cause you to dwell in this place"*[101]. Next, Jeremiah addresses their erroneous belief that **God's temple** promised them unconditional immunity. He says,

> *Jeremiah 7:4*
> *"Trust you not in lying words, saying, The temple of YeHoVaH, The temple of YeHoVaH, The temple of YeHoVaH, are these."*

Then, Jeremiah specifies the root of the problem, namely, their behaviour.

> *Jeremiah 7:5-10*
> *"For if you thoroughly amend your ways and your doings; if you thoroughly execute judgment between a man and his neighbour; [If] you oppress not the*

---

[99] *Isaiah 29:13 "Wherefore the Lord said, Forasmuch as this people draw near me with their mouth, and with their lips do honour me, but have removed their heart far from me, and their fear toward me is taught by the precept of men:"*
[100] Verse 3
[101] Verse 3

*stranger, the fatherless, and the widow, and shed not innocent blood in this place, neither walk after other gods to your hurt: Then will I cause you to dwell in this place, in the land that I gave to your fathers, for ever and ever. Behold, you trust in lying words, that cannot profit. Will you steal, murder, and commit adultery, and swear falsely, and burn incense unto Baal, and walk after other gods whom you know not; And come and stand before me in this house, which is called by my name, and say, We are delivered to do all these abominations?"*

Jeremiah hit hard and direct at the problem's root. He specified the conditions under which God promised His people could live safely in Jerusalem. It was not as they thought. Rather, their protection hinged on their obedience to doing what God required of them, not simply the temple's presence in Jerusalem. Unfortunately, the bulk of the people neither received Jeremiah, his words, nor his wisdom.

Meanwhile, in Babylon, Ezekiel contended with the Jews there for they, like those in Jerusalem, clung to that same mindset. To help them break free of that mindset, YeHoVaH gave Ezekiel an illustration to present to the Babylonian captives.

Chapter 9
A Deadly Defence

## AHOLAH AND AHOLIBAH[102]

As the parable opens, God speaks of two sisters. In relating their life's story, He discusses their background, ensuring the listeners knew that both sisters came from the same mother[103]. As God explains the sister's history, He mentions their roots in Egypt, for it was there that their idolatry began, that which YeHoVaH described as whoredoms. He relates their names:

**Aholah, the elder and Aholibah, the younger. Samaria is Aholah and Jerusalem, Aholibah.**

During the process of time, Aholah plays the harlot. YeHoVaH speaks of her doting devotion for her many lovers. He highlights their appeal to Aholah through their glamorous appearance which included displays of royal splendour and gallantry. He makes it clear that Aholah never abandoned her idols of Egypt and therefore was never faithful to Him.

YeHoVaH gave her over to what her heart desired, *the Assyrians.* These abused her, robbed her and eventually slew her with the sword. In the end, she became renowned among women because they *(the*

---

[102] This illustration comes from *Ezekiel 23:1-49*.
[103] The covenant relationship with God began with the mother. God was faithful to their seed.

*Assyrians)* executed judgment upon her. In other words, due to her life, her behaviour, her end and the reason for it, Aholah became famous[104].

Next, God moves on to discuss her younger sister, Aholibah. He begins by mentioning that Aholibah knew about her sister's end and the reason for it. However, the tragic end of Aholah's life did not carry any weight with her. Instead, Aholibah poured herself into her idolatry (whoredoms) even more than her sister. Her inordinate acts of love intensified in number and in strength, far surpassing her sister.

In response to her behaviour, YeHoVaH says, that "His mind was alienated from her[105] as His mind was from her sister". Yet, this did not stop Aholibah. She ignored the warning and increased her whoredoms. Responding to Aholibah's resistance to Him, and to help her to repent and return to Him, God promised to turn her lovers against her. Additionally, God delivered her into the hand of the ones she hated; the ones from whom she alienated her mind, Babylon.

Yet, for all this Aholibah did not stop her whoredoms. Therefore, God promised that Aholibah would drink of the same cup as her sister. He concludes His

---

[104] Summary of *Ezekiel 23:1-10*.
[105] *Ezekiel 23:18*

## Chapter 9
## A Deadly Defence

promises with this statement, *"Because you have forgotten Me, and cast Me behind your back, therefore you bear your lewdness and whoredoms[106]."*

Following that statement, YeHoVaH invites his listeners to judge Aholah and Aholibah[107]. He reiterates their adultery against Him. YeHoVaH then recounts their further sins including the times when they gave their sons dedicated to YeHoVaH, to die in the fires of Molech. After doing that abomination, they then came into His temple on the sabbath to worship Him without any remorse for their disobedience. Thus, they profaned His sanctuary and polluted His sabbaths. YeHoVaH continues to list specifics which offended Him including things brought into His house to further defile it.

YeHoVaH concludes that the righteous men will judge both Aholah and Aholibah as lewd, adulterous women. As the parable ends, the crime for that form of adultery received the death penalty. With that, their lewdness ceases in the land.

---

[106] Ezekiel 23:35

[107] Death was the punishment for adultery. *Leviticus 20:10 "And the man that committeth adultery with another man's wife, even he that committeth adultery with his neighbour's wife, the adulterer and the adulteress shall surely be put to death."*

YeHoVaH then closes the illustration with three powerful statements:
- *A lesson learned* from the parable, *"that all women may be taught not to do after their lewdness"*[108].
- *Payment for sins* must happen. Regarding Judah, she refused to repent and return to God. Therefore, she bore the punishment of her idolatry.
- *YeHoVaH's final comment* concludes with this statement: *And you shall know that I am YeHoVaH"*[109].

After bringing forth this illustration, the children of Israel in Babylon had opportunity to identify the sin which highly offended God.

Moreover, they would know that *due to that idolatry, God would not spare the temple in Jerusalem from destruction nor Judah from captivity.* They saw this as God's direct hand and began to turn away from the idolatry that took them into Babylon[110].

---

[108] *Ezekiel 23:48*

[109] *Ezekiel 23:49*

[110] Jewish history shows that Israel, after her exit from Babylon, no longer engaged in the same idolatry as before her exile.

Chapter 9
A Deadly Defence

## IDOLATRY'S CONCLUSION

Remember our question, *"How can a people given so much, including victory over their enemies from the hand of God, become participants in the very abominations, which God used them to remove"*.

A simple answer lies in the bottom line of the parable of Aholah and Aholibah. Aholah, like Aholibah did the same thing, namely satisfy themselves. When the older sister's sins manifested sooner and her end came for Aholibah to see, Aholibah refused to take a lesson from her sister. This happened mostly because these sisters established their own code of behaviour, not measuring it against the commands of God. Additionally, both fell prey to the guise of deception which presents good as evil and evil as good.

*Isaiah 5:20-21*
> *"Woe unto them that call evil good, and good evil; that put darkness for light, and light for darkness; that put bitter for sweet, and sweet for bitter! Woe unto them that are wise in their own eyes, and prudent in their own sight!"*

Deception, *in this case as in others*, works hard to build a defensive wall. It clads that wall with the armour of erroneous thinking, giving its victims permission to ignore God's standards of normal. Instead, it exchanges God's ideals of right and wrong for the world's definition, removing any idea of God's penalties. It then defines those new concepts and ideals as normal and promises appealing rewards. In this manner, deception builds a deadly resistance to truth, protecting it a false sense of security.

In other words, deception says, *"if you do the same things, what bad things happened to others will not happen to you"*. Deception intends to effectively cover up the idea of sin. It will not admit sin exists, nor even hint on any reflection of sin. Deception expels the need to closely examines one's actions and bars out any idea of wrongdoing. This topic Proverbs addresses:

*Proverbs 28:13*
*"He that covers his sins shall not prosper: but whoso confesses and forsakes them shall have mercy."*

In the parable of Aholah and Aholibah, rather than admit to the sin which the Word of God clearly stated, deception took it in at another direction. Deception veered their eyes away from seeing idolatry as spiritual adultery. Additionally, deception blocked out the penalty of any form of adultery, spiritual or otherwise. It closed the door to repentance and opened the door to death.

## Chapter 9
## A Deadly Defence

Deception, with its tentacles sunk deep into its victims, forwarded the world's agenda, and both Aholah and Aholibah kept their sin, lured by their lusts.

*1 John 2:15-16*
*"Love not the world, neither the things [that are] in the world. If any man love the world, the love of the Father is not in him. For all that [is] in the world, the lust of the flesh, and the lust of the eyes, and the pride of life, is not of the Father, but is of the world."*

Both sisters were drawn to elaborate, royal apparel and its lifestyle[111], desirable young men[112], captains, rulers, great lords and renowned[113], and other things which the world propagated as goodly.

In the end, the traps and snares of the world captured their heart, and so they hardened it to the things of God. Of this same thing, Jeremiah speaks:

*Jeremiah 7:25-28*
*"Since the day that your fathers came forth out of the land of Egypt unto this day I have even sent unto you all my servants the prophets, daily rising up early and sending them: Yet they hearkened not unto me, nor*

---

[111] *Ezekiel 23:5-7*
[112] *Ezekiel 23: 12-16*
[113] *Ezekiel 23:22-23*

*inclined their ear, but hardened their neck: they did worse than their fathers. Therefore you shall speak all these words unto them; but they will not listen to you: you shall also call unto them; but they will not answer you. But you shall say unto them, This is a nation that obeys not the voice of YeHoVaH their God, nor receiveth correction: truth is perished, and is cut off from their mouth."*

It is better to perceive the world and its entrapments as scripture relates:

1 John 2:17
*"And the world passeth away, and the lust thereof: but he that doeth the will of God abideth for ever."*

To avoid deception's wall of resistance which holds tight to the things of this world, let us recognize deception's tactics. Let us press into God and ask Him to help us keep our thinking aligned with scripture.

**May our helmet of salvation guard our minds and hearts. May we hold high our shield of faith. As we wield the sword of the Spirit, may we cut through every one of deceptions deadly defences so not even the tiniest trace of deceit touches our life.**

# 10

*A Passionate Pursuit*

*"Look unto me, and be you saved, all the ends of the earth: for I am God, and there is none else."*

Isaiah 45:22

**JUDAH'S SINS MATCHED** those of Northern Israel. Under the reign of King Manasseh of Judah, the crimes against the God of heaven soared. In fact, history looks at the acts of Manasseh and presents him as the most evil king to ever sit upon Israel's throne. Nevertheless, Manasseh during his reign, when caught in a desperate situation, cried out to YeHoVaH and received from Him great mercy. We will discuss that event and God's mercy later, but first, let us consider the wicked deeds of King Manasseh, noting why history calls him Israel's most evil king.

*2 Kings 21:1-2*
*"Manasseh was twelve years old when he began to reign, and reigned fifty and five years in Jerusalem. And his mother's name was Hephzibah. And he did that which was evil in the sight of YeHoVaH, after the abominations of the heathen, whom YeHoVaH cast out before the children of Israel."*

In the opening verses of 2 Kings, the author gives us the age of Manasseh[114] when he ascended the throne and gives us the years that he reigned[115]. Then, it summarizes the manner of Manasseh's rule, calling his behaviour evil in the sight of YeHoVaH. After that, it begins to explain those evils and continues to list them to verse 9. Below is a summary of those verses:

**MANASSEH'S EVIL DOINGS:**

| #  | EVIL | 2 Kings 21: |
|----|------|-------------|
| 1. | Went after the abominations of the heathen. | Verse 2 |
| 2. | Built again the high places that his father Hezekiah removed. | Verse 3 |
| 3. | Reared up the altars for Baal. | Verse 3 |
| 4. | Made a grove (for Baal worship). | Verse 3 |
| 5. | Worshipped and served the host of heaven. | Verse 3 |

---

[114] Age 12
[115] Ruled for 55 years.

| | | |
|---|---|---|
| 6. | Built altars for the hosts of heaven in the two courts of YeHoVaH, (in His House). | Verse 4-5 |
| 7. | Made his sons pass through the fire (offered to Molech.) | Verse 6 |
| 8. | Observed times and used enchantments. | Verse 6 |
| 9. | Dealt with familiar spirits and wizards. | Verse 6 |
| 10 | Set a graven image of the grove that he made in the house of YeHoVaH. | Verse 7 |
| 11 | Manasseh seduced Israel to do more evil than did the evil nations whom YeHoVaH destroyed before the children of Israel | Verse 9 |

2 Kings 21 goes on with its list of evils, summarizing what God decided to do regarding those evils. At the end, it gives a general summary of Manasseh's sins:

*2 Kings 21:10-16*
*"And YeHoVaH spake by his servants the prophets, saying, Because Manasseh king of Judah has done these abominations, and has done wickedly above all that the Amorites did, which were before him, and has made Judah also to sin with his idols: Therefore thus said YeHoVaH God of Israel, Behold, I am bringing such*

*evil upon Jerusalem and Judah, that whosoever heareth of it, both his ears shall tingle. And I will stretch over Jerusalem the line of Samaria, and the plummet of the house of Ahab: and I will wipe Jerusalem as a man wipes a dish, wiping it, and turning it upside down. And I will forsake the remnant of my inheritance, and deliver them into the hand of their enemies; and they shall become a prey and a spoil to all their enemies; Because they have done that which was evil in my sight, and have provoked me to anger, since the day their fathers came forth out of Egypt, even unto this day. **Moreover, Manasseh shed innocent blood very much, till he had filled Jerusalem from one end to another; beside his sin wherewith he made Judah to sin, in doing that which was evil in the sight of YeHoVaH."***

A sister account of Manasseh in 2 Chronicles 33, adds the following:

2 Chronicles 33:9-10
*"So Manasseh made Judah and the inhabitants of Jerusalem to err, and to do worse than the heathen, whom YeHoVaH had destroyed before the children of Israel. And YeHoVaH spake to Manasseh, and to his people: but they would not listen.*

## Chapter 10:
## A Passionate Pursuit

YeHoVaH, through His prophets, spoke to Manasseh and to his people. Unfortunately, they refused to listen. Therefore, in response to the unrepented sins of Manasseh and his people, YeHoVaH sent the captains of the hosts of the king of Assyria[116] to war against Jerusalem. They took Manasseh captive, bound him with fetters, put a hook and chain in his nose, and carried him off to Babylon.

### DECEPTION'S STRONGHOLD ON MENASSEH

Deception overtook Menasseh as he passionately pursued evil. Under deception's grasp, Menasseh dishonoured the House of YeHoVaH, offered his sons to Molech, sought counsel from wizards and those with familiar spirits, and worshipped the hosts of heaven.

Some even claim Menasseh gave the orders for the prophet Isaiah's execution[117]. Whether that is true or not, Menasseh had blood on his hands for the many lives lost to the fires of Molech and for the furtherance of idolatry in Judah and Jerusalem. Menasseh even defiled the house of God in a manner no one ever did before him[118].

---

[116] Babylon at that time was a vassal city under the control of Assyria, not yet taken by Nebuchadnezzar.

[117] The Bible is silent on that matter.

[118] As we look at what restitution Menasseh made, it identifies some of the evils Menasseh did to defile God's house.

However, during Menasseh's captivity, deception's grip was broken, showing ample proof of God's ability to break through the greatest darkness and restore a repented soul to Himself.

## DECEPTION'S PASSIONATE PURSUIT BROKEN
2 Chronicles 33 gives us the story.

> *2 Chronicles 33:12-13*
> *"And when he was in affliction, he besought YeHoVaH his God, and humbled himself greatly before the God of his fathers, And prayed unto him: and he was intreated of him, and heard his supplication, and brought him again to Jerusalem into his kingdom. Then Manasseh knew that YeHoVaH he was God."*

While in captivity, Menasseh implored YeHoVaH to help him. Humbling himself before YeHoVaH, the God of his fathers, Menasseh returned his heart to God. YeHoVaH heard Menasseh and with a move of His hand brought Menasseh back home to Jerusalem. Fortunately, Menasseh had learned from his time in captivity, and he not only repented, but he made efforts to restore the devastation that he caused to the house of God, also to Judah.

> *2 Chronicles 33:14-20*
> *"Now after this he built a wall without the city of David, on the west side of Gihon, in the valley, even to*

## Chapter 10:
## A Passionate Pursuit

*the entering in at the fish gate, and compassed about Ophel, and raised it up a very great height, and put captains of war in all the fenced cities of Judah. And he took away the strange gods, and the idol out of the house of YeHoVaH, and all the altars that he had built in the mount of the house of YeHoVaH, and in Jerusalem, and cast them out of the city. And he repaired the altar of YeHoVaH, and sacrificed thereon peace offerings and thank offerings, and commanded Judah to serve YeHoVaH God of Israel. Nevertheless, the people did sacrifice still in the high places, yet unto YeHoVaH their God only. Now the rest of the acts of Manasseh, and his prayer unto his God, and the words of the seers that spake to him in the name of YeHoVaH God of Israel, behold, they are written in the book of the kings of Israel. His prayer also, and how God was intreated of him, and all his sin, and his trespass, and the places wherein he built high places, and set up groves and graven images, before he was humbled: behold, they are written among the sayings of the seers. So Manasseh slept with his fathers, and they buried him in his own house: and Amon his son reigned in his stead."*

After his return, Menasseh strengthened the fortifications of Jerusalem, as well as tried to undo some of the evil which he had done. He removed the strange gods, and the idol out of the house of YeHoVaH. He removed the altars that he had built in the mount of the house of YeHoVaH, and in Jerusalem, and ensured they were carried out of the city.

Additionally, Menasseh saw to the repair of the brazen altar of YeHoVaH. That altar Menasseh personally used as he personally made peace and thank offerings to YeHoVaH on that altar. Moreover, Menasseh commanded Judah to serve YeHoVaH, the God of Israel. These acts became evidence with a physical confirmation that Menasseh held a genuine repentance for his evil doings and returned to YeHoVaH. Scripture confirms this fact saying that *"Menasseh knew that YeHoVaH was his God[119]"*.

## GOD'S COMPASSIONATE MERCY

Throughout these many chapters of this book, we discussed the numerous tactics of deception. We did that to bring awareness so these tactics might be avoided. Moreover, we highlighted events in people's lives who lived under deception's grip, a grasp from which they never broke free.

We read of wicked kings who died in their wickedness. Then, in this chapter, we read of the most wicked king of all, Menasseh. We hear of his many atrocities

---

[119] *2 Chronicles 33:13 "And prayed unto him: and he was intreated of him, and heard his supplication, and brought him again to Jerusalem into his kingdom.* **Then Manasseh knew that YeHoVaH he was God."**

## Chapter 10:
## A Passionate Pursuit

against God, but we noted that he humbly bows before the Almighty and beseeches Him. YeHoVaH in His mercy responds and Menasseh's chains break. His life of bondage ends. Then, his prison doors open and this king returns to the city of Jerusalem from where he came, back to the city which he loves.

Deception presents a formidable image with powerful strongholds; however, the prayer of a sincere individual sees deception's strongholds shattered, its grip broken and its sense of reality altered. In the case of Menasseh, it was not by a powerful, face to face, encounter with God; nor was it by one of God's prophets standing before the king. Rather, Menasseh's release from captivity came through God's mercy, by way of a sincere cry from his repented heart. His earnest cry reached the one and only God who could save him: The God of Abraham, Isaac and Jacob, YeHoVaH!

Much earlier, when Solomon dedicated the temple to God, he prayed a powerful prayer for mercy, too:

*1 Kings 8:46-52*
*"If they[120] sin against you, (for there is no man that sins not,) and you be angry with them, and deliver them to the enemy, so that they carry them away captives unto*

---

[120] God's people.

*the land of the enemy, far or near; Yet if they shall bethink themselves in the land whither they were carried captives, and repent, and make supplication unto you in the land of them that carried them captives, saying, We have sinned, and have done perversely, we have committed wickedness; And [so] return unto you with all their heart, and with all their soul, in the land of their enemies, which led them away captive, and pray unto you toward their land, which you gave unto their fathers, the city which you have chosen, and the house[121] which I have built for your name: Then hear you their prayer and their supplication in heaven your dwelling place, and maintain their cause, And forgive your people that have sinned against you, and all their transgressions wherein they have transgressed against you, and give them compassion before them who carried them captive, that they may have compassion on them: For they [be] your people, and your inheritance, which you brought forth out of Egypt, from the midst of the furnace of iron: That your eyes may be open unto the supplication of your servant, and unto the supplication of your people Israel, to listen unto them in all that they call for unto you."*

---

[121] We do not know whether Menasseh prayed towards the house of God in Jerusalem or not, but the bulk of the prayer, nevertheless, applies.

## Chapter 10:
## A Passionate Pursuit

Solomon, as he prayed this prayer under the guidance of the Holy Spirit, laid out some powerful principles of repentance. Additionally, YeHoVaH verified His acceptance of this prayer when He lit the sacrifice offered along with this prayer.

> 2 Chronicles 7:1-3
> "Now when Solomon had made an end of praying, the fire came down from heaven and consumed the burnt offering and the sacrifices; and the glory of YeHoVaH filled the house. And the priests could not enter into the house of YeHoVaH, because the glory of YeHoVaH had filled YeHoVaH's house. And when all the children of Israel saw how the fire came down, and the glory of YeHoVaH upon the house, they bowed themselves with their faces to the ground upon the pavement, and worshipped, and praised YeHoVaH, [saying], For [he is] good; for his mercy [endureth] for ever."

As we end this chapter and this section, let us rejoice as we recognize the great mercy of God on those caught in deception's ruthless grip. Let us treasure the awesome heart of God Who willingly embraces a repented heart.

Additionally, let us honour God with our prayers for those caught in deception's grip. We know how His hand of mercy touches those repented souls, removes their bondages and set them totally free.

**Such is the mercy of the Saviour, the God we serve!**

*Furthermore, let us remember that no matter how one passionately pursued evil in their lifetime, if they sincerely repent, God hears from heaven. If they are willing to forsake it all and follow Him, a new life awaits!*

John 3:16
"For God so loved the world, that he gave his only begotten Son, that whosoever believeth in him should not perish, but have everlasting life."

# DECEIVED

## Section 3: Deception Conquered

*In the last section*, we examined first covenant examples of people whose lives showed us some of deception's tactics. As we ended that section, we peered into the life of one man held deeply in deception's grip, Manasseh. Then, we saw how God broke deception's grasp when Manasseh repented.

*In this section*, we begin by another first covenant example, however, this life shows us a life dedicated to serving the God of Abraham, Isaac and Jacob, YeHoVaH.

# 11

### A Righteous Relationship

*"Now therefore arise, O YeHoVaH God, into your resting place, you, and the ark of your strength: let your priests, O YeHoVaH God, be clothed with salvation, and let your saints rejoice in goodness. O YeHoVaH God, turn not away the face of your anointed: remember the mercies of David your servant."*

2 Chronicles 6:41-42

**JOSIAH, KING OF ISRAEL** came to the throne at eight years of age. According to the account of his life in the book of Kings, Josiah did that which was right in the sight of YeHoVaH.

> 2 Kings 22:2
> "And he did that which was right in the sight of YeHoVaH, and walked in all the way of David his father, and turned not aside to the right hand or to the left."

King Josiah, in the 18th year of his reign, at the age of 26, decided to see the temple repaired. Since repairs cost money, Josiah sent a certain scribe, Shaphan, with instructions to speak with the high priest, Hilkiah. Josiah spoke with Hilkiah and following the King's order, told him to sum up the silver collected regularly from the people's giving. Afterwards, Hilkiah was to release the total amount to those who oversaw the care of God's house. They were to buy the materials they needed for the repairs and pay for the carpenters, builders, masons and other craftsmen hired to restore the house.

Hilkiah followed the king's orders. In his search to collect the silver throughout the house of God, he found a book of the Torah[122]. Immediately, the book was taken and read to the king. As Josiah heard the scripture, he understood that the many atrocious practices operating in Israel, God classified as sin and consequently, their disobedience earned God's wrath. In grief, he tore his garments, a sign of deep grief in Israel at that time. Next, king Josiah sent to inquire of God as to what would happen to him and all Judah.

---

[122] There are five books in the Torah. Hilkiah found one of the five. Scholars conclude this was the book (scroll) of Deuteronomy that Hilkiah discovered. A further explanation of the reasons it was thought to be the book of Deuteronomy follows later in the main chapter content.

## Chapter 11
### A Righteous Relationship

> *2 Kings 22:11-13*
>
> *"And it came to pass, when the king had heard the words of the book of the law, that he rent his clothes. And the king commanded Hilkiah the priest, and Ahikam the son of Shaphan, and Achbor the son of Michaiah, and Shaphan the scribe, and Asahiah a servant of the king's, saying, Go you, enquire of YeHoVaH for me, and for the people, and for all Judah, concerning the words of this book that is found: for great is the wrath of YeHoVaH that is kindled against us, because our fathers have not hearkened unto the words of this book, to do according unto all that which is written concerning us."*

Huldah, the prophetess, brings them God's response:

> *2 Kings 22:15-20*
>
> *"And she said unto them, Thus said YeHoVaH God of Israel, Tell the man that sent you to me, Thus said YeHoVaH, Behold, I will bring evil upon this place, and upon the inhabitants thereof, even all the words of the book which the king of Judah has read: Because they have forsaken me, and have burned incense unto other gods, that they might provoke me to anger with all the works of their hands; therefore my wrath shall be kindled against this place, and shall not be quenched. But to the king of Judah which sent you to enquire of YeHoVaH, thus shall you say to him, Thus said YeHoVaH God of Israel, As touching the words which*

*you have heard; Because your heart was tender, and you have humbled yourself before YeHoVaH, when you heard what I spake against this place, and against the inhabitants thereof, that they should become a desolation and a curse, and has rent your clothes, and wept before me; I also have heard you, said YeHoVaH. Behold therefore, I will gather you unto your fathers, and you shall be gathered into your grave in peace; and your eyes shall not see all the evil which I will bring upon this place. And they brought the king word again."*

God gave mercy to Josiah because his heart was tender towards God, and he humbled himself before Him. However, the people of Israel forsook God, burned incense unto other gods, and provoked God to anger with their abominations. Consequences from the actions of the people, unrepented were warranted. God's wrath still burned and could not be quenched.

## GOD'S WRATH UNQUENCHED
Regarding the fact of God's wrath not being quenched, *while we read of the atrocities of the Jews, which kindled His wrath,* we do not hear of *any form or action towards repentance from the people.* Throughout the records of the Bible, which gives an historic account of Josiah's life, we do not hear mentioned the Day of Atonement, Yom Kippur, when Israel repented and atoned for their sin.

## Chapter 11
## A Righteous Relationship

Throughout its content, Deuteronomy addresses sins which offend God, especially those which follow the faith practices of the gods of their enemies in the land, however while it speaks of Passover, it does not speak of the day of atonement. Josiah, extremely grieved over the sins of Israel, throughout his reign never practiced the Day of Atonement, neither did many other kings before and after Josiah. This is one reason why scholars believe the book discovered in Josiah's time was that of Deuteronomy.

Regarding sin, Deuteronomy says:

*Deuteronomy 12:28-32*
*"Observe and hear all these words which I command you, that it may go well with you, and with your children after you for ever, when you do [that which is] good and right in the sight of YeHoVaH your God. When YeHoVaH your God shall cut off the nations from before you, whither you go to possess them, and you succeed them, and dwell in their land; Take heed to yourself that you be not snared by following them, after that they be destroyed from before you; and that you enquire not after their gods, saying,* **How did these nations serve their gods? even so will I do likewise. You shall not do so unto YeHoVaH your God**[123]*: for every abomination to YeHoVaH, which he*

---

[123] One does not take practices done to other gods and bring them to YeHoVaH, doing the same thing. YeHoVaH has specific

*hate, have they done unto their gods; for even their sons and their daughters they have burnt in the fire to their gods. What thing soever I command you, observe to do it: you shall not add thereto, nor diminish from it."*

These things the people of Israel practiced. They enquired after foreign gods, observed their religious practices, or adopted those practices in the worship of YeHoVaH. Moreover, they gave their sons and daughters to be burnt in the fire[124]. These practices, which were done in Israel, explains the deep grief that overtook Josiah when he heard the reading of Deuteronomy[125].

Additionally, Josiah commanded a Passover celebration[126], but no mention is made of the Day of Atonement[127]. Again, Deuteronomy discusses the Passover extensively, which again explains why Josiah commanded the Passover be celebrated. However, as

---

requirements, and it is within those requirements His people must serve Him. *"Whatsoever I command you, observe to do it: you shall not add thereto nor diminish from it."* Deuteronomy 12:32

[124] A practice to Chemosh and Molech.

[125] This is but one of the passages in Deuteronomy which addresses sins and their consequences.

[126] 2 Kings 23:23 *"But in the eighteenth year of king Josiah, wherein this Passover was held to YeHoVaH in Jerusalem."*

[127] Day of Atonement holds the sacrifice for forgiveness of sins of the priest and the people of Israel.

mentioned earlier, the book of Deuteronomy does not discuss the Day of Atonement. If the book discovered had spoken of the Day of Atonement, assuredly Josiah would have commanded its practice. So, while Josiah repented and God forgave him, no repentance nor atonement came from or behalf of the people, therefore God's wrath remained unquenched.

## JOSIAH'S REIGN

As Josiah's reign continued, he did much to restore God's house and to remove idolatry from the land. Until the day of his death he was faithful to YeHoVaH[128]. Below is a list of some major things the Bible tells us that Josiah did in Israel.

## DEEDS OF JOSIAH

| # | GOOD WORK | 2 Kings 22: |
|---|---|---|
| 1. | Repaired the house of YeHoVaH. | Verse 4-7 |
| 2. | Repented & sought God on behalf of himself and for his people. | Verse 13-20 |
| | | 2 Kings 23 |
| 3. | Gathered the elders of Jerusalem, men of Judah and inhabitants of Jerusalem, (priests, prophets, all people great and small) to hear the | Verse 1-2 |

---

[128] *2 Chronicles 35:20-23*

book of the law they found and had it read to the people.

4. Made a covenant with God to walk after Him, to keep His commandments, testimonies, and statutes with their heart, soul and strength and to perform the words of the covenant written in the book. — Verse 3

5. Commanded to bring out all the vessels made for Baal that were in YeHoVaH's house. He removed those images placed in the grove for all the host of heaven. He had the grove uprooted and burned in the Kidron Valley. — Verse 4, 6

6. Put down all the idolatrous priests, removing them from their service in high places in Judah, and round about Jerusalem. — Verse 5

7. Stopped incense to Baal, the sun, the moon, the planets, and to all the host of heaven. — Verse 5

8. Broke down the houses of the sexual offenders[129]. — Verse 7

---

[129] KJV uses the word sodomites, but translators, in believing they understand the intentions, use the term shrine/cult prostitutes, or sexual offenders.

## Chapter 11
### A Righteous Relationship

9. Removed the priests who burned incense to Baal from Jerusalem. — Verse 8
10. Defiled of all the high places where the priests burned incense from Geba to Beersheba. — Verse 8
11. Broke down the gates of the high places that were in the gate of the governor of the city. — Verse 8
12. Defiled Topheth in the valley of Hinnom so no one could be offered to Molech. — Verse 10
13. Removed the horses and burned the chariots dedicated to the sun. — Verse 11
14. Removed altars made by the kings of Judah, including any remnants of Manasseh's altars in the courts of the house of YeHoVaH. — Verse 12
15. Removed high places before Jerusalem near mount of corruption, built by Solomon which included abominations dedicated to Ashtoreth, Chemosh and Milcom and defiled them. — Verse 13
16. Broke in pieces the images in the groves and cut down the groves in places inside and outside of Jerusalem. — Verse 14

| | | |
|---|---|---|
| 17. | Broke down the altar and high place at Bethel[130] built by Jeroboam[131]. | Verse 15 |
| 18. | Josiah took away all the houses of the high places in the cities of Samaria. | Verse 19 |
| 19. | Commanded the people to keep the Passover. | Verse 21 |
| 20. | Put away the workers with familiar spirits, the wizards, the images and idols, and all the abominations that he spied out in Judah and Jerusalem. | Verse 24 |
| | | 2 Chronicles 35 |
| 21. | Told Levites to put the Ark of the Covenant back into the House of YeHoVaH, restored the courses of the priests, commanded them to sanctify themselves and to do all | Verse 3 to 6 |

---

[130] Thus, he fulfilled the word of YeHoVaH as given in *1 Kings 13:2* "*And he cried against the altar in the word of YeHoVaH, and said, O altar, altar, thus said YeHoVaH; Behold, a child shall be born unto the house of David, Josiah by name; and upon you shall he offer the priests of the high places that burn incense upon you, and men's bones shall be burnt upon you.*"

[131] Josiah, in his exuberance to remove corruption from Israel, went into territory formerly designated to Northern Israel. That kingdom ceased to exist under King Hezekiah, and so no longer was in existence during the reign of King Josiah.

## Chapter 11
## A Righteous Relationship

|  |  |
|---|---|
| according to the word of YeHoVaH which came through Moses. | |
| 22. Restored the singers and the porters to the house of YeHoVaH. | Verse 15 |

A study of Josiah's life makes it clear that he did not fall into deception, however, his life was not perfect. An incident near the end of his life indicates a weakness in his ability to discern a particular matter, which in the end caused his death.

*2 Chronicles 35:20-24*
*"After all this, when Josiah had prepared the temple, Necho king of Egypt came up to fight against Carchemish by Euphrates: and Josiah went out against him. But he sent ambassadors to him, saying, What have I to do with you, you king of Judah? [I come] not against you this day, but against the house wherewith I have war: for God commanded me to make haste: forbear you from [meddling with] God, who [is] with me, that he destroy you not. Nevertheless Josiah would not turn his face from him, but disguised himself, that he might fight with him, and hearkened not unto the words of Necho from the mouth of God, and came to fight in the valley of Megiddo. And the archers shot at king Josiah; and the king said to his servants, Have me away; for I am sore wounded. His servants therefore took him out of that chariot, and put him in the second chariot that he had; and they brought him to Jerusalem,*

and he died, and was buried in [one of] the sepulchres of his fathers. And all Judah and Jerusalem mourned for Josiah."

We can understand the reason why Josiah might not receive the words from Necho. However, under such circumstances it is amazing that Josiah never sought a prophet of God regarding the battle. In the end, Josiah died having been wounded by an arrow.

In looking at his life, however, we can learn many things from Josiah. Below are seven things.

1. When Josiah was 8 years old, he began to seek God, learning to walk in the ways of what pleased God[132].
2. He made a covenant with God on behalf of himself and God's people[133].
3. He thought restoration of God's house and its system of worship a priority and saw to its

---

[132] 2 Chronicles 34:1-3 "Josiah [was] eight years old when he began to reign, and he reigned in Jerusalem one and thirty years. And he did [that which was] right in the sight of YeHoVaH, and walked in the ways of David his father, and declined [neither] to the right hand, nor to the left. For in the eighth year of his reign, while he was yet young, he began to seek after the God of David his father: and in the twelfth year he began to purge Judah and Jerusalem from the high places, and the groves, and the carved images, and the molten images."
[133] 2 Chronicles 35:32

## Chapter 11
## A Righteous Relationship

    completion, including a provision of finances to fund the restoration[134].

4. He put God's word as a priority in his life, honoured it, and lived for it with all his heart[135].
5. He set a good example for others by following the commands of God. He adapted these in his personal life as well as in his governmental role as king[136].
6. He set the singers and worshippers in place in the house of YeHoVaH. This restoration speaks of his desire for YeHoVaH to be honoured as well as worshipped[137].
7. As the ruler of Israel, he determined to see that the nation, which God called to be a light to the world, to function in the way God desired. That function included the removal of the horrible atrocities added to the worship of YeHoVaH, such the worship of idols, images, and the killing of babies through the worship of Molech[138].

For sure, many more lessons can be gained by studying the life of King Josiah. As we look at his life, we see

---

[134] *2 Kings 22:3-7*
[135] An overview of his activities from *1 Kings and 2 Chronicles*.
[136] An overview of his activities from *1 Kings and 2 Chronicles*.
[137] *2 Chronicles 35:3-6*
[138] An overview of his activities from 1 Kings and 2 Chronicles.

principles for walking correctly with God. Adapting those principles to Christian living today, such as a passion for hearing the word of God and obeying it, gives a clear understanding of how to live a life without deception's pull. Indeed, applying wisdom from Josiah's life keeps deception a long way off.

Before we close this chapter, let us look at Josiah's life and what he did to overcome the patterns of deception such as those we studied in section two of this book. Doing so will give us a quick glimpse into how Josiah defeated deception.

| Title: A Shrouded Scheme |
|---|
| Josiah did not surrender to Baalim's error of mixing or mingling customs or covenants of the land with his faith *(nor into his governmental role as did Solomon)*. Josiah had a desire for his people to walk with God in a pure faith. We see that in his concern for cleansing the land from idolatry. |
| Title: A Destined Disaster |
| Josiah did not succumb to the thinking of his day. Instead, he clung to the Word of God as he knew it, doing his best to follow its precepts. He kept God's Word as his moral compass and swerved not away from it. |

## Title: A Deceptive Devotion

Josiah, unlike Saul, knew that he could not decide for God. As king, he did not do whatever he liked. He humbled himself before God and obeyed God. Josiah had no fear of his opponents nor their opinions. He set about to do the work of YeHoVaH keeping his heart aligned with truth.

## Title: A Sinister Snare

Josiah, unlike King Solomon, gave no room for idolatry in his life and thus he gave a powerful example to his nation as he lived out his life before them. Josiah walked the straight and narrow path described in scripture.

## Title: A Corrupted Counsel

Josiah, unlike Jeroboam, did not set up worship systems designed to keep him as king. Rather, Josiah sought counsel from God's appointed sources and thus, with his alignment with scripture, was used of God to return the worship system to its origin, ensuring only what God ordained for His house remained in the house.

## Title: A Perilous Partnership

Josiah did not make any covenants with those outside of Israel, and within Israel, he held no strange partnerships. Unlike Ahab, Josiah embraced no foreign gods, nor any women who worshipped them. Josiah held no perilous partnerships.

## Title: A Deadly Defence

Josiah's priority was God, his house, his laws, commands and statutes. He did not buy into the system of the world around him during his time, nor alter his course to suit people of influence around him. Instead, Josiah, as a powerful leader, became the example and walked in a righteous manner for others to see.

## Title: A Passionate Pursuit

Josiah, unlike Manasseh, walked away from every ungodly thing. He hated the same things that God hated and loved the things God loved, things shown by the life of king David. This included such things as God's Word, praise and worship to the King of Kings. Additionally, Josiah respected God's ordained prophets[139] and listened to them.

As we end this review on Josiah's life, we close with a scripture summarizing his life:

*2 Kings 23:25*
*"And like unto him was there no king before him, that turned to YeHoVaH with all his heart, and with all his soul, and with all his might, according to all the law of Moses; neither after him arose there any like him."*

---

[139] In the case of *2 Kings 22:14* it was a woman, the prophetess, Huldah, which delivered the Word of YeHoVaH to the king.

Chapter 11
A Righteous Relationship

In this brief recap of Josiah's life, we see the benefits of honouring God, of making Him a priority, and of applying faith principles into every avenue of our life, including the vocation to which God appoints us. We recognize, wholeheartedly, the benefits of Josiah's righteous relationship with God.

*"Unto You, O YeHoVaH, do I lift up my soul. O my God, I trust in You: let me not be ashamed, let not my enemies triumph over me. Yea, let none that wait on You be ashamed: let them be ashamed which transgress without cause. Show me Your ways, O YeHoVaH; teach me your paths."*
*Psalm 25:1-4*

*Lord, help us to long for Your truth in all things and to align our lives accordingly. Help us to respect Your commands, precepts, and statutes like Josiah and walk in the manner suitable to the covenant people You created in Yeshua.*

# 12

*A Corrected Course*

*"He has shewed you, O man, what is good; and what does YeHoVaH require of you, but to do justly, and to love mercy, and to walk humbly with thy God?"*

*Micah 6:8*

**W**HEN LOOKING AT ISRAEL in Biblical times, we receive insight as to what God required of those who claim YeHoVaH as their God. Seeing Israel, then, acting in her role as the light to all nations, we see her receiving a divine course correction to walk in alignment with truth.

On the flip side, when Israel dramatically steered her ship with the rudder of self-will, doing whatsoever she willed, her light dimmed. She then displayed herself as a nation out of alignment with God and truth. During those times we get a glimpse into the harsh reality of a chosen people who refused to walk in alignment with YeHoVaH's righteous decrees.

Throughout scripture, then, as it records Israel's history with YeHoVaH, alongside Israel's actions, we see God's heart as He responds to His chosen nation. Let us take a quick review of Israel's need for correction, looking for undertones of YeHoVaH's heart in the matter.

## ISRAEL UNDER MOSES

At Mount Sinai the nation received its charter, religious and governmental laws. Through these things we get to know YeHoVaH's righteous decrees for a nation called to walk in oneness with Him. However, for that oneness to happen, Israel needed to modify her behaviour and thus shed the ways she absorbed while in Egypt. That oneness required a powerful realignment, a corrected course to walk with Him. As YeHoVaH, through Moses, released His righteous commandments, statutes, and precepts as well as His ordained feast days for the people to follow, some obeyed, while others did not.

To align with God, therefore, and walk as one with Him, God required Israel's obedience. It also required faith in Him. In the forty years Israel walked in the desert, we hear about their lack of faith. That faith was as simple as remembering the parting of the Red Sea, the bitter water changed at Meribah[140]; the defeat of the

---

[140] *Exodus 17:6-7 "Behold, I will stand before you there upon the rock in Horeb; and you shall smite the rock, and there shall come water out of it,*

## Chapter 12
## A Corrected Course

giants, the Amalekites, at Rephidim[141]; the regular feeding with manna; as well as the other visible actions shown to Israel by their all-powerful God.

Those who aligned their belief with God's truth prospered, and those who failed to do so, never entered His rest and missed the promised land.

*Psalm 95:10-11*
*"Forty years long was I grieved with this generation, and said, It is a people that do err in their heart, and they have not known my ways: Unto whom I swore in my wrath that they should not enter into my rest."*

### ISRAEL UNDER JOSHUA

Later, Israel, under the leadership of Joshua, prospered as most of the people aligned their faith with that of their leader. However, these people needed a course correction, as among them was a man named Achan[142]. Achan allowed greed to override his sense of duty. This greed overpowered his faith to follow God's

---

*that the people may drink. And Moses did so in the sight of the elders of Israel. And he called the name of the place Massah, and Meribah, because of the chiding of the children of Israel, and because they tempted YeHoVaH, saying, Is YeHoVaH among us, or not?"*
[141] *Exodus 17:8-16*
[142] *Joshua 7:1 "But the children of Israel committed a trespass in the accursed thing: for Achan, the son of Carmi, the son of Zabdi, the son of Zerah, of the tribe of Judah, took of the accursed thing: and the anger of YeHoVaH was kindled against the children of Israel."*

commands. In the end he and his family died while the faithful others received their reward inside the Promised Land.

## ISRAEL UNDER JUDGES

In the time of Judges, as we read in this book, people did what they thought was right in their own eyes. These people constantly grieved God and regularly required a course correction. First, they needed to recognize their misdirected affections, so God allowed their daily life to reap the penalty of their unfaithfulness to Him. When they faced the result of those choices, they cried out to God. He sent them a deliverer. As that deliverer remained alive, they did well, but once the deliverer died, they walked out of alignment with truth once again. That cycle repeated itself continually.

## ISRAEL UNDER KING DAVID

Under King David, a man after God's own heart, both people and God seemed content. David set a good example of one who aligned his life with truth Although the Bible shows an incident of David's disobedience, he repented immediately once he understood his error[143]. God rewarded both king and country for their obedience to Him. During David's time, he desired to build God a house where He could

---

[143] *2 Samuel 2:1-15*

dwell. God denied David that privilege but gave it to his son, Solomon.

## ISRAEL UNDER SOLOMON

Solomon began his reign following in the footsteps of his father David. He put his shoulder to the task of building God a magnificent House. Unfortunately, early in Solomon's reign, he walked out of alignment with the covenant God of Israel and made a covenant with Pharoah and sealed it with his marriage to the daughter of Pharoah. He brought her to Israel, expanded his building projects which included a house for his wife and for her gods[144].

As Solomon's life continued, he allowed his misalignment with truth to continue. Thus, he shifted off course, refused to repent and receive any course correction. In the end, Solomon degraded to worshipping false gods, an action which deeply offended God. As a result, God promised to divide the kingdom of Israel after Solomon's death.

## ISRAEL AS A DIVIDED KINGDOM

Israel became two kingdoms, just as God promised. Israel in the North he gave to Jeroboam, and Judah and Jerusalem to Rehoboam. While Judah and Jerusalem remained in alignment with truth for a time, Northern

---

[144] *1 Kings 7:8; 2 Chronicles 8:11*

Israel, from the beginning entered a misalignment with truth. This happened because Jeroboam, the man God chose to lead the nation, did not retain his faith in God, nor hold to the promises God gave to him. Jeroboam designed a faith system in misalignment with truth. This system set a new course for Northern Israel from which they never recovered.

Many kings sat on the throne of Northern Israel for a little over the 200 years of their existence. Every one of them walked out of sync with God, embracing the false system of worship set up by Jeroboam. Thus, no king that ever sat on the throne of Northern Israel did the Bible record as being a good king, doing right in God's eyes. In other words, no king of Northern Israel ever received a course correction and realigned with truth. Consequently, God ended that nation and scattered its people to the ends of the earth.

Judah and Jerusalem lasted about 350 years. In that time, they had 20 kings. Of those 20 kings only 8 kings did right in the sight of YeHoVaH[145]. In this book, we only looked at one king who did right, Josiah. In reviewing his life, we noted that he aligned himself with the word of God and did not allow himself to go to either the right of the left. He, like most good kings, aligned his life with truth and thus, his name falls into

---

[145] A quick reference from Google.com.

the category of those kings who the Bible says, did right in the eyes of YeHoVaH.

## JUDAH AFTER THE RETURN

While we haven't covered it in this book, after God scattered the southern kingdom of Judah, He brought them back to the land of Israel and to the city of Jerusalem. When this part of Israel returned, her rulers became governors but never ruled as kings. Some governors like Zerubbabel were good rulers who aligned with God's word, but others were not. Yet each generation faced decisions to align with truth or to live their lives by their own standards.

As Israel progressed, the priests took a more powerful role in leading the nation. Under Zadok's descendants, the priests aligned with the principles of God's kingdom. Around the time of the Maccabeans, the priesthood shifted and became corrupt. As the time came closer to the coming of Messiah, (Yeshua/Jesus), the priesthood became misaligned with truth. This was one issue Yeshua addressed at His coming as He spoke to the Pharisees, Sadducees and others.

## ISRAEL AFTER YESHUA

Many years after Yeshua's death, burial and resurrection, Rome destroyed Jerusalem. Israel, as a nation, ceased to exist with her peoples scattered throughout the face of the earth. However, in 1948

Israel became a nation one more time. Just like before, Israel became centre stage for all nations to watch. Today, with the modern state of Israel, the president, prime minister and Knesset (government) operate as her leadership. Some of these individuals align with the scriptures in their personal and political lives, while others to not.

## ACCOUNTABILITY TO GOD

No matter how one looks at an alignment with truth, (a course correction) whether it is regarding Israel or not, there is no getting away from the fact that God judges all nations and all people [146] on their choices. This fact exemplifies a powerful bottom line here in that God requires individuals to align with truth.

To put it another way, when asked what God requires, Malachi, the prophet, said, that people should "do justly, love mercy and walk humbly with Elohim[147]. Alignment with YeHoVaH's standards of righteousness becomes a necessary course correction which no person nor nation can avoid. Consequently, all people in every nation of the world, *eventually*, give account to God for their choices.

---

[146] *Joel 3:1-21; Matthew 25:31-46*
[147] *Micah 6:8 "He has shewed you, O man, what is good; and what does YeHoVaH require of you, but to do justly, and to love mercy, and to walk humbly with thy God?"*

Chapter 12
A Corrected Course

## GOD'S REACIONS TO DECEPTION

Throughout this book, we looked at deception and the part it played in misleading God's people. At times, we saw God's merciful hand bless the leaders which followed Him. Conversely, we saw God's reactions, although still merciful, as He responded negatively when leaders turned their backs on Him, and embraced idolatry. Idolatry, of course, invited God's corrective hand upon Israel, both on individuals as well as upon the nation. However, in our study thus far, we have *not* looked at how idolatry affected God.

*Deuteronomy 32:21*
*"They have moved me to jealousy with that which is not God; they have provoked me to anger with their vanities: and I will move them to jealousy with those which are not a people; I will provoke them to anger with a foolish nation."*

Idolatry moved God to jealousy. It provoked Him to anger. In fact, in the same scripture that tells us these facts, exposing the root of problem of the people which provoked Him. God says it was *"their vanities"*. Vanities, biblically speaking, refers to that which is empty, such as "in the context of worldly pursuits and human endeavours disconnected from God" [148]. A literal translation of the biblical word, הֶבֶל indicates a

---

[148] Result of a search on Google.com to describe the biblical word vanity.

breath, or vapour. Something that is very illusive and temporary.

| Strong's # | Hebrew word | Pronunciation |
|---|---|---|
| 1892 | הֶבֶל | hebel<br>heh'bel |
| Interpreted as vanity, vain, or at times, altogether. |||

One, however, can see the vapour idea of vanity, easily in the Hebrew pictograph word:

| Hebrew | Symbol | Possible Meanings |
|---|---|---|
| *Parent Root:* |||
| הֶ | Man with outstretched arms | Behold, breath, awesome, surrender. |
| בֶ | Tent door | Door, doorway, entrance way, gate, etc. |
| *Parent Root Picture* || *A breath that enters in.* |
| *Child Root* |||
| לֶ | Shepherd's staff | Authority, control, pull toward, etc. |
| *Child Root Picture* || *To control.* |
| **Overall Meaning** |||
| A breath that enters inside to control. (Comment: A breath has no substance and consequently, can bring no substance.) |||

## Chapter 12
## A Corrected Course

In other words, something falling in the biblical definition of the word vanity, brings emptiness for it flees away like a wind or like someone's breath. Its goal is to take the person to nothing, to total emptiness. This fits well with the scripture in Ecclesiastes:

*Ecclesiastes 1:2*
   *"Vanity of vanities, said the Preacher, vanity of vanities; all is vanity."*

Considering their vanities as the root problem, *as mentioned in Deuteronomy 32:21*, those vanities pointed to an empty, unfulfilled existence. **Widely paraphrasing** the first part of *Deuteronomy 32:21*, it **might read**:

*"They have moved me to jealousy taking to themselves that that which is not Me; they have provoked me to anger when they replaced Me, (Who is life), with that which brings them to emptiness (or death)."*

To put it another way, the space (or God void) that God created in humankind for Himself so that humankind would have life, they try to fill with other things which have no value. What futility! Add to this the fact that idolatry carries with it a spiritual application, and you have another good reason why this provoked God to anger! It took His beloved creation to their spiritual death while God preferred, they had life. God hated that end for their sakes.

*Deuteronomy 32:15-18*

*"But Jeshurun[149] waxed fat, and kicked: you are waxen fat, you are grown thick, you are covered with fatness; then he forsook God which made him, and lightly esteemed the Rock of his salvation. They provoked him to jealousy with strange gods, with abominations provoked they him to anger. They sacrificed unto devils, not to God; to gods whom they knew not, to new gods that came newly up, whom your fathers feared not. Of the Rock that begat you, you are unmindful and have forgotten God that formed you."*

Often when Israel was blessed by God, enjoying and growing fat on those blessings, they forsook God, and *"lightly esteemed"* (foolishly disregarded) the Rock of their salvation. Their relationship with strange gods provoked God to jealousy, and to anger. In explaining this action, God clearly states, *"they sacrificed unto devils, not to God, to gods whom they knew not, to new gods which newly came up, which their fathers knew not"*. They gave God no mind and forgot the very one that formed them.

God, in His infinite wisdom and understanding, knew the exact fruit of a life glued to vanity, to emptiness, another trap of deception. He also knew the inabilities of such gods to provide for His people. They were

---

[149] Another name for Israel.

## Chapter 12
## A Corrected Course

vanity, empty and fleeting. They have no ability to do what only He could do. It was God that sent the rain. It was the true and living God that created and sustained the fatness of the land which the people enjoyed. It was God on whom the people turned their backs.

Worship and honour for these provisional realities they enjoyed came from God and God alone. Therefore, it was His love for them and their destined end which they could not see that provoked Him when they offered sacrifices to devils, and worshipped gods that were no gods. In the end, their life would be fruitless and empty just like the gods they chose to worship.

YeHoVaH, the God of Abraham, Isaac and Jacob is so loving and caring, such actions moved Him to jealousy and anger because He saw the results of their choices. To help them recognize their vanities and come out of agreement with them, He turned them over to that which they wanted.

As a result, they tasted and experience the emptiness, and then, remembering the good fruit they enjoyed earlier with YeHoVaH, they could repent and return to Him. Thus, those who chose to repent, their latter choice would be their better choice!

## GOD'S RESPONSE TO HIS PEOPLE'S RETURN

As God's people return to Him[150], surely, He rejoices over them to do them good and blesses them with good things.

*Deuteronomy 30:9*
*"And YeHoVaH your God will make you plenteous in every work of your hand, in the fruit of your body, and in the fruit of your cattle, and in the fruit of your land, for good: for YeHoVaH will again rejoice over you for good, as he rejoiced over your fathers:"*

Furthermore, He treats His people as they never left Him, giving restoration and further promises of blessings.

*Psalm 68:8-13*
*"Among the gods there is none like unto You, O YeHoVaH, neither are there any works like unto Your works. All nations whom You have made shall come and worship before You, O Lord; and shall glorify Your name. For You are great and do wondrous things: You are God alone. Teach me Your way, O YeHoVaH; I will walk in Your truth: unite my heart to fear Your name. I will praise You, O Lord my God, with all my heart: and I will glorify Your name for evermore. For great is Your mercy toward me: and You have delivered my soul from the lowest hell."*

---

[150] Or any new person seeks His face and comes to Him.

Chapter 12
A Corrected Course

**DECEPTION DEFEATED**

Anyone snared by deception's devices, unknowingly follows a dangerous path. Their life, its goals and treasures pull them to an unfulfilled life, a life of *emptiness*. However, their call to God, opens a door to a life which prospers them, and gives to them a hope and expected end[151].

Regarding the fulness God promises:

> 1 Corinthians 2:9
> "But as it is written, Eye has not seen, nor ear heard, neither have entered into the heart of man, the things which God has prepared for them that love him."

So great is YeHoVaH's love for humankind that He desires to spring deception's many snares and set its victims free. Thus, He extends an open door to know Him, or in the case where deception carried away one *who once knew Him*, His open arms await their return. All it takes is genuine repentance and a sincere desire to walk with Him.

Deception, which acts as a god, cannot resist or retain in its grasp on any who long to know the truth. To

---

[151] Jeremiah 29:11 *"For I know the thoughts that I think toward you, said YeHoVaH, thoughts of peace, and not of evil, to give you an expected end."*

such a one who cries out to Him, He will make a way for them to escape the grasp of deception. Once the heart focuses on knowing truth and willingly aligns with it, deception receives a blow of defeat from which it cannot recover.

While we have not covered the New Covenant in this book, it is worth mentioning that the apostles, Paul and Peter, issued letters with minor course corrections to straying believers. Interesting enough, the book of Revelation speaks of Christian assemblies needing a course correction too, some for the idolatry. For example, the church in Pergamos embraced Baalim's error:

> *Revelation 2:14*
> *"But I have a few things against you, because you have there them that hold the doctrine of Balaam, who taught Balac to cast a stumblingblock before the children of Israel, to eat things sacrificed unto idols, and to commit fornication."*

Additionally, the church in Thyatira followed the deception of Jezebel.

> *Revelation 2:20-21*
> *"Notwithstanding I have a few things against you, because you suffer that woman Jezebel, which calleth herself a prophetess, to teach and to seduce my servants to commit fornication, and to eat things sacrificed unto*

## Chapter 12
## A Corrected Course

*idols. And I gave her space to repent of her fornication; and she repented not."*

These scriptures, as well as others throughout the New Covenant, strongly indicate that the same deceptions as faced by first covenant saints can be experienced by second covenant saints. It is a broad deception tactic to think otherwise.

In closing this chapter, let us keep focused on defeating and overcoming deception. It is very possible to do so because of the God Whom we serve. How awesome is His love. How amazing is His ability, when trusted, to bring to pass true life's fulfillment and eternal happiness to humankind.

Our part requires listening for His input regarding any needed course correction. Surely, asking Him to help us walk within His plans and purposes for our life, brings fulfillment in every avenue of our being, including a course correction. Let each one of us, no matter our relationship with Him, remain open to receive even the slightest course correction and thus, live to walk in truth and glorify His Name.

*"Hear my cry, O God; attend unto my prayer. From the end of the earth will I cry unto You, when my heart is overwhelmed: lead me to the rock that is higher than I. For You have been a shelter for me, and a strong tower from the enemy. I will abide in Your tabernacle for ever: I will trust in the covert (secret place) of Your wings. Selah."*

*Psalm 61:1-4*

*Father, as we sail through this life with You, may we always give you the helm. May we remember Your unfailing love for us which desires the best for us. As we move towards our unforeseen days in the future, may our confidence be in You and Your ability, not in our own understanding, wisdom or strength. Keep us attentive to the voice of Your Holy Spirit, willing to align with any corrected course required.*

*Amen*

*Conclusion*

*"But the hour cometh, and now is, when the true worshippers shall worship the Father in spirit and in truth: for the Father seeketh such to worship him. God [is] a Spirit: and they that worship him must worship [him] in spirit and in truth."*

*John 4:23-24*

**D***eception, as this book revealed*, masks itself in many ways. Its goal, no matter the means it uses, reaches to destroy. Deception falls into the category of ha satan's tools:

John 10:10
*"The thief comes not, but for to steal, and to kill, and to destroy: I am come that they might have life, and that they might have [it] more abundantly."*

Knowing this about deception, prepares us for the times in our life when deception tries to knock on our door. As it does, let us keep alert to some of the main points discussed in this book.

## A Shrouded Scheme

Remember Baalim's error, designed to creep in slowly and change things ever so slightly! Let us watch for areas where subtle off course changes might try to come in. Let us watch as ha satan tries to mix lies, half truths and the like into our life through any accessible area. In short, let us refrain from mixing God's perfect principles with the devices of the world.

## A Destined Disaster

Let us ensure we keep God and His Word as a priority. Let us ensure that His light is that which guides us in all our choices. One good measuring stick comes by weighing our choices on the balance scale of what is right in God's eyes, and not only in that of our own eyes or of another's. Let us examine the fruit of our choices to ensure its rooted in the Holy Spirit's wisdom and not our own.

## A Deceptive Devotion

Let us ensure our life's choices fall within a single eye devotion to God and His truth. Let us remember to acknowledge God's commands, laws and ideals. God still sees them as applicable in our modern world. Additionally, let us heed them for His Word, like the Author[152], never changes.

---

[152] *Hebrews 13:8 "Jesus Christ the same yesterday, and today, and for ever."*

## Conclusion

### A Sinister Snare

This chapter spoke of idolatry. Idolatry defines as anything that shifts, moves, or replaces God's place in our lives. Let us not forget that idolatry tries to change one's focus, adjusting it little by little, to redirect its victim to other sources. Idolatry's root, remember, stems from vanity, or emptiness. Idolatry, no matter the form it takes, aims to turn the heart away from God. Let us be on guard for modern forms of idolatry.

### A Corrupted Counsel

This is where God's wisdom must be sought, for the Bible describes one's heart as desperately wicked. While salvation changes the attitude of the heart, believers should still guard their heart for deception's snare. Therefore, let us be on guard for misquotes, misdirects, or manipulations aimed to take one in a direction opposite to the counsel of God.

### A Perilous Partnership

Influential connections in life come at any time. In today's day and age, such connections include internet as well as social media influences. Let us be mindful of things of influence sown in our life, which intentionally or unintentionally, aim to pull us off course. It can happen to the very young. It can happen to the very old and anyone in between. None are immune.

## A Deadly Defence

Let us be alert to that which scripture declares as unrighteous but the world around us presents as normal. In such circumstances, when we stick to Biblical righteousness, accusations may come when one refuses to participate in ungodly activities, but the wisdom and strength of God await all who ask. In this case, our best defence is to stand on the side of God and not shift from that place in Him.

## A Passionate Pursuit

Remember Manasseh! Remember Solomon. Their lives speak loudly of powerful individuals with great influence that did whatsoever please them.

- *Solomon* played with fire by embracing idolatrous women. At first, he put their worship at a distance from him, but in the end of his life, he worshipped the same false gods as his wives. We never hear of Solomon's repentance.
- *Manasseh,* as King of Israel, brought idolatry to a new height in Judah. He worshipped these idols and even participated in giving human sacrifices to Molech. Manasseh, when in great distress repented and was given opportunity to make some restitution, however, his evil works and their effects on others he could not change.

Let us ensure our passionate pursuit focuses on the things of God.

## CLOSING COMMENTS

Having walked through these many chapters on the topic of deception, we conclude by reminding the reader of the length of this study which unfortunately, could not accommodate all that deception brings forward, nor every way to defeat it. Its traps are innumerable. However, through these pages, we were able to bring an awareness of deception's existence, the knowledge of which gives one a powerful line of defence.

Additionally, we refer to another powerful defence, one which time did not allow to cover earlier. That defence we find outlined in the book of Revelation. Here we receive an important concept for defeating ha satan, his plans and many deceptions:

*Revelation 12:11*
*"And they overcame him by the blood of the Lamb, and by the word of their testimony; and they loved not their lives unto the death."*

One cannot over emphasize the value of Yeshua's precious blood and its application in a believer's life. Along side the blood, of course, comes the word of their testimony, a life which aligns with truth, willing to follow it even unto death.

Let us never forget the precious blood of Yeshua. Let us hold fast to the pattern for living for it applies to every generation. Let us cling to the scriptures and never depart from their counsel.

*"The law of YeHoVaH is perfect, converting the soul: the testimony of YeHoVaH is sure, making wise the simple."*

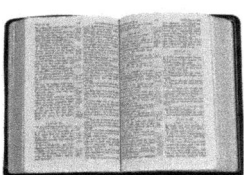

*Psalm 19:7*

**Be aware! Be wise! Be ready!**

# APPENDIX

# A Name to Honour
# יְהֹוָה
# YeHoVaH[153]

If, today, someone asked you to tell them the name of your earthly father, without hesitation you would declare it. If, for some reason, you did not know the identity of your earthly father, you would say so. You might even give an explanation as to why that might be so. Thus said, if asked to relate the name of your heavenly Father, today, would you do so with ease, or would you draw a blank?

Most of Christendom, today, is ignorant *as to the name of the Father*, as well as the way to pronounce it. As the author of this book, I would like to join the ranks of those who wish to relate that name to the world. I believe that when we stand before the Father on the day that we give an account for our deeds in this body, it would be a good thing to know His Son, His Name!

---

[153] Based on information given by Michael Rood. Some from his work entitled, The Chronological Bible, and some from his YouTube videos. For more information see page 28 of the Chronological Bible.

## About The Name

Did you know that the name of the Father appears at least 6,828 times in the Hebrew scriptures? Scribes recorded it with four specific Hebrew letters. They are as follows:

| | |
|---|---|
| י | Pronounced yode, or yod |
| ה | Pronounced as hey |
| ו | Pronounced as vav |
| ה | Pronounced as hey |

For centuries, whenever the Jews come across these 4 letters they simply say, Adonai, or Ha Shem (meaning the name). They refuse to pronounce the name for several reasons, some of which we will look at momentarily. For now, let us look at whether their tradition affected Christianity. That we can easily do by looking at our Bibles to see the 4-letter name of the Father either written or substituted.

A quick look reveals that our KJV Bibles, as well as many other versions, the 4-letter name presented to readers is a 4-letter English word, "YeHoVaH". [154] [155] Whether intentional or not, Christendom has followed the ancient tradition of the Jews.

---

[154] In some translations it is GOD.
[155] We also can shorten that name to YHVH (Yod, Heh, Vav, Heh)

## An Ancient Tradition

In early second century times[156] Rabbis hid the pronunciation of the holy name of God. They did this by omitting the vowel pointings, which are necessary to make the name pronounceable. Hence, as they carefully wrote the scriptures, their omittance of the vowel pointings made the name unpronounceable. Historians believe there were two reasons why they did this:

    i.    According to Josephus, Rome, under the rule of Domitian, 81 to 96 CE, put to death anyone using the name of the Jewish or Christian God.

    ii.   Many believe that the Rabbis borrowed a tradition from pagans, whereby the name of their god was considered too holy to mention, so they called him "Ba-al" meaning Lord. The Jews adopted this practice and most still practice it today, even some Messianic Jews!

## Tradition Continues

Bible translators followed their tradition for many reasons which are not presently known. It is possible, they forgot the pronunciation of the name, but more than likely, those who knew it, hid it.[157] Whatever the reason, following this tradition caused Christians to continue in this tradition.

---

[156] Some scholars even dating further back.
[157] According to some, the Jews secretly knew the name.

*Does that tradition offend the Heavenly Father?*
If indeed its origin was Baal worship, then we can give a resounding Amen to the fact it offends God. In addition, as we look at scripture, we see the Apostle, Peter, declaring that "whosoever shall call upon the name of YHVH[158] shall be saved.[159]" Clearly God desires that all, including the Gentiles, come to Him[160] for salvation.

## An Historic Discovery

Today, some Hebrew scholars[161] have searched the world over for Hebrew manuscripts. In doing so, they found many Hebrew documents have the full name with vowels and therefore the pronunciation of the name. These scholars may different slightly in pronunciation, but nevertheless, they are making the name of YeHoVaH known today.

## Our Saviour's Name Hidden in This Name

In looking at the Hebrew root of the name of the Father, pronounced *Yah-Ho **Vah'***, and looking at

---

[158] In a moment you will see that YHVH's Name is in our Saviour's Name.

[159] *Joel 2:32; Acts 2:21*

[160] If they call upon the name of YJVH, surely the Father will show them Yeshua! *Romans 10:12-15*

[161] Nehemiah Gordon, a Hebrew scholar, according to his testimony on his website continues to mention increasing numbers of incidents in manuscripts where the name of God with all vowel appointments appears.

another scripture, we see something amazing about our Saviour. In speaking of the Prophet, the one the Father would send and to whom all must listen and obey, YeHoVaH said that His name would be in the name of the Prophet.

*Exodus 23:21 "Beware of him, and obey his voice, provoke him not; for he will not pardon your transgressions[162]: for my name [is] in him".*

**Our Saviour's name, as given by the angel was "Yehoshua", which means Salvation.**

That name, with its Hebrew letters reads as:

| | |
|---|---|
| י | **Pronounced yode or yod** |
| ה | **Pronounced hey** |
| ו | **Pronounced vav** |
| שׁ | Pronounced shin |
| ע | Pronounced ayin |

The name of the Father (יְהֹוָה) is in the name of the Son! The first three letters of YeHoVaH show it! (Yod, Heh, Vav). Is it so amazing that the name of our Father is in the true name of the One YeHoVaH sent to redeem us!

---

[162] Please keep in mind that Yeshua bore the punishment for your sins. Your sins were not pardoned in the sense no punishment was paid. Yeshua atoned for them on your behalf!

## Honour the Father's Name

Throughout this book, and all later books, as well as all accompanying audios and PowerPoints, it is the author's intention to widely use, proclaim and continually pronounce the name of the Father, as well as the name of Yeshua. Indeed, this breaks with tradition of many, however, thus far as we have shared the news of the Father's name and use Yeshua's birth name, reception has been excellent.

## Name Challenge

Since, as of this reading, you are no longer ignorant of your heavenly Father's name, we invite you to join the unofficial network of proclaimers of the Father's name and shout it from the house tops. In doing so, you honour the Heavenly Father, our Savour Yeshua, and the Holy Spirit.

> *Romans 10:12-15*
>> *"12 For there is no difference between the Jew and the Greek: for the same Lord over all is rich unto all that call upon him. 13 For whosoever shall call upon the name of YeHoVaH shall be saved. 14 How then shall they call on him in whom they have not believed? and how shall they believe in him of whom they have not heard? and how shall they hear without a preacher? 15 And how shall they preach, except they be sent? as it is written, How beautiful are the feet of them that preach the gospel of peace and bring glad tidings of good things!"*

## ABOUT THE KING JAMES VERSION

Scriptures quoted in this book *originate* from the KJV **public domain version** of the Bible, which means, no copyright exists on this version of the scripture. While some find this translation outdated, Jeanne, trained in the KJV still finds this version helpful, and uses it in all her books[163].

In using KJV, however, it is good to remember the following:
- Some words in the KJV have changed meaning over the centuries. To understand such words, look up the root word in its original language. In doing so, the meaning stands out. For example. KJV uses the word "conversation" however, in its original language it means moral character, or behaviour.
- When KJV spoke of humanity, they said, "mankind". When you read that word, or hear others speak about the scriptures using the term, "mankind", know it refers to all humankind, not a specific gender.

Due to tradition, the name of the Father, YeHoVaH appears as LORD, or at times as Jehovah. However, in all Jeanne's manuscripts, YeHoVaH or YHVH replaces the term LORD.

---

[163] In later manuscripts, the author updated the more archaic words in the KJV such as wouldest or couldest.

## SALVATION'S MESSAGE

Yeshua, when walking on earth, said this:
> John 3:14-18
>> *14 And as Moses lifted up the serpent in the wilderness, even so must the Son of man be lifted up: 15 That whosoever believes in him should not perish but have eternal life. 16 For God so loved the world, that he gave his only begotten Son, that whosoever believes in him should not perish, but have everlasting life. 17 For God sent not his Son into the world to condemn the world; but that the world through him might be saved. 18 He that believes on him is not condemned: but he that believes not is condemned already, because he has not believed in the name of the only begotten Son of God.*

During the time of Moses, the children of Israel in the wilderness, rebelled against God, at which time poisonous serpents infiltrated the camp, killing many of the people. After seeking YeHoVaH for a solution to the problem, Moses followed God's instructions and made a bronze serpent fashioned and erected it on a pole in sight of the people. Whosoever wanted to live, must acknowledge their rebellion against YeHoVaH, and in doing so, look upon the erected pole and bronze serpent, to YeHoVaH, who gave them life in place of death, then they would live.

Yeshua said, just as Moses erected that bronze serpent in the wilderness, He would be lifted for all to see. This referred to the event, in the future, of Yeshua's crucifixion. During the time when the serpent hung on that pole, whosoever wanted to live and not die from the serpent's bite must acknowledge their rebellion, their sin against YeHoVaH.

Likewise, for those who wish to live eternally, they must look upon the cross of the crucified One, to Yeshua, who provided life for them. This was an act of love for all humankind, necessary because man is born from Adam, and thus is born with an inherent sin.

Secondly, man sins. The consequence of sin is death, and eternal death, wherein man will spend an eternity in darkness, away from YeHoVaH. Unfortunately, there is nothing humanly possible to reverse those consequences. Even if a person had made a genuine decision never to sin again, and for some reason they succeeded, all their good deeds and good living would not erase the penalty of eternal death.

There is only *one way* for Eternal Life to touch a person's life. That way, Yeshua explained to His listeners, comes *through the cross.*

Salvation comes by understanding these facts:

1. Yeshua, being the Son of God and the fulfilment of the scriptures, never sinned.
2. YeHoVaH, on behalf of every human being on the earth, chose to make Yeshua become as sin, in His Eyes, so that Yeshua might pay the penalty for sin, for all of humanity.
3. Yeshua paid that penalty. He died on the cross and was buried in a tomb.
4. Three days later, He rose again, appearing to His disciples, to show them the reality of His resurrection, to show them God vindicated Him and made Him both Lord and Messiah.
5. Yeshua could not stay in the tomb, because "death" comes to all who sin, but since Yeshua never sinned, therefore, death could not hold Him in the grave.
6. All those who come to Yeshua, to receive Him as their Saviour, receive liberty from sin and from its horrible consequence, eternal death.
7. They enter YeHoVaH's Kingdom and receive eternal life, as well as another gift: The Righteousness of Messiah. After salvation, when YeHoVaH looks upon a believer in Messiah, He sees Yeshua's perfect life and sees a redeemed believer, set aside for YeHoVaH. Since salvation has taken place in the believer, the Holy Spirit dwells within them.
8. All it takes to receive salvation from YeHoVaH is receiving His Messiah, fully repenting from

sinning against God[164]. YeHoVaH even gives the believer the faith to receive His gift of Salvation!

The Apostle Paul put it this way:

*Ephesians 2:8*
   *"For by grace are you saved through faith; and that not of yourselves: it is the gift of God"*

When you pray the following prayer, realize we present it here to get you started in your walk with YeHoVaH. Living out your salvation depends upon your commitment to follow through *from this point, onward*. From the moment of your commitment and onward, dear one, please seek YeHoVaH for His help in all things, including help to make your life align with truth, and in the end be a praise unto His name, forever!

---

[164] *And against man. When a person steals, etc. they sin against both God and man. PLEASE NOTE: all references to "man", either by scripture or the author, refers to all humankind, not a specific gender.*

## SINNER'S PRAYER & LIFETIME COMMITMENT

Heavenly, Father:
I acknowledge before You, YeHoVaH, that I am a sinner. I understand sin's punishment is a life without You, for all eternity. Thank You for sending Yeshua to the earth, as the Messiah. I understand now that He died in my place, to take my punishment for my sins. I believe You raised Yeshua from the dead, and now that I accepted Him as my personal Saviour, my old life dies, and my new life begins.

I humbly ask You to forgive me of my sins, and as of this moment, I receive Yeshua as my Saviour. I open my heart to receive the works of the cross that You provided for me through Yeshua, and with Your help, I will walk away from my sin, turning my back upon my own will and ways. I will now live my life seeking to obey Your Word and Your will. Help me to live, from this point onward, in a manner pleasing to You.

*One more thing:*
Remember, this gospel message comes with power. When you hear it, the Kingdom of God draws near to you. When you repent of your sins and receive Salvation, the Kingdom of God moves within. You cannot see it, feel it, or tell it from an outward observance. It is accepted, received, and lived out by faith! Seek out other believers in Messiah and may

God bless you richly as you live your life, now, completely for Him!

**So now, be sure and tell someone!**

Remember that a person believes with the heart unto righteousness and confesses with their mouth unto salvation, as spoken about in *Romans 10:10"*:
>  *"10 For with the heart man believes unto righteousness; and with the mouth confession is made unto salvation*

# SCRIPTURE INDEX

## 1

*1 Chronicles 10:13-14* . 80
*1 Chronicles 16:15-17* . 22
*1 Corinthians 1:10* ...... 40
*1 Corinthians 2:9* ...... 199
*1 Corinthians 3:16* ...... 35
*1 John 1:8-10* ............... 77
*1 John 1:8-10.* ............... 45
*1 John 2:15-16* ........... 151
*1 John 2:15-17* ............. 61
*1 John 2:3-6* ................. 45
*1 Kings 11:11-12* ....... 101
*1 Kings 11:1-4* ........... 103
*1 Kings 11:28* ............ 111
*1 Kings 11:30-31* ....... 111
*1 Kings 11:31-32* ....... 111
*1 Kings 11:33* ............ 113
*1 Kings 11:3-40* .......... 105
*1 Kings 11:37-38* ....... 112
*1 Kings 11:39-36* ....... 109
*1 Kings 11:4* ................ 96
*1 Kings 11:4 b* ............. 95
*1 Kings 11:4-8* ............. 94
*1 Kings 11:9* .............. 100
*1 Kings 11:9-10* ........... 96
*1 Kings 12:16-20* ....... 116

*1 Kings 12:20* ............ 117
*1 Kings 12:22-24* ....... 116
*1 Kings 12:26-27* ....... 119
*1 Kings 12:26-32* ....... 118
*1 Kings 12:4* ............... 115
*1 Kings 12:6-14* .......... 115
*1 Kings 13:2* ............... 176
*1 Kings 14::7-16* ........ 118
*1 Kings 14:21-24* ....... 139
*1 Kings 14:2-4* ........... 119
*1 Kings 16:25-26* ....... 123
*1 Kings 16:28-30* ....... 124
*1 Kings 16:31-33* ....... 124
*1 Kings 17:1* .............. 131
*1 Kings 18:10* ............ 135
*1 Kings 18:12-14* ....... 127
*1 Kings 18:17* .... 128, 134
*1 Kings 18:18* .... 128, 134
*1 Kings 18:18 b)* ........ 134
*1 Kings 18:19* ............ 129
*1 Kings 18:36-39* ....... 130
*1 Kings 18:41* ............ 131
*1 Kings 18:6-11* ......... 126
*1 Kings 19:18* ............ 125
*1 Kings 20:13,22,38* .. 133
*1 Kings 22:7* .............. 133
*1 Kings 3:12-14* ........... 98
*1 Kings 3:1-3* ............... 93

1 Kings 3:7-9 ............... 97
1 Kings 7:8 ......... 101, 189
1 Kings 8:46-52 .......... 161
1 Kings 9:2-9 ............... 99
1 Peter 1:16 .................. 39
1 Samuel 10:23 ............ 84
1 Samuel 12:19-25 ...... 73
1 Samuel 15:10-12 ...... 85
1 Samuel 15:18-21 ...... 86
1 Samuel 15:22-23 ...... 87
1 Samuel 15:24-26 ...... 87
1 Samuel 15:27-28 .... 111
1 Samuel 15:7-9 .......... 84
1 Samuel 2:17; 24 ........ 74
1 Samuel 28:7 ............... 80
1 Samuel 31:1-8 .......... 88
1 Samuel 6:1 ................. 75
1 Samuel 8:11 a ........... 89
1 Samuel 8:11-12 ........ 82
1 Samuel 8:13 ............... 83
1 Samuel 8:15 ............... 83
1 Samuel 8:16 ............... 83
1 Samuel 8:17 ............... 83
1 Samuel 8:18 ............... 83
1 Samuel 8:4-5 ............. 81
1 Samuel 8:6-9 ............. 81

## 2

2 Chronicles 33:12-13 158

2 Chronicles 33:13 .... 160
2 Chronicles 33:14-20 158
2 Chronicles 33:9-10 . 156
2 Chronicles 34:1-3 ... 178
2 Chronicles 35:20-23 173
2 Chronicles 35:20-24 177
2 Chronicles 35:3-6 ... 179
2 Chronicles 6:41-42 . 167
2 Chronicles 8:11 ...... 189
2 Kings 21:10-16 ....... 155
2 Kings 21:1-2 ........... 154
2 Kings 22:11-13 ....... 169
2 Kings 22:14 ............ 182
2 Kings 22:15-20 ....... 169
2 Kings 22:2 .............. 167
2 Kings 22:3-7 ........... 179
2 Kings 23:23 ............ 172
2 Kings 23:25 ............ 182
2 Peter 2:14-16 ............ 62
2 Peter 3:9 .................. 133
2 Samuel 2:1-15 ........ 188
2 Timothy 2:19-21 ...... 39

## A

Acts 2:21 .................... 214
Amos 8:11 .................. 132

## D

Daniel 11:32 b ........... 232

*Deuteronomy 11:16-17* ............................... 125
*Deuteronomy 11:22-25* 91
*Deuteronomy 12:30* .. 204
*Deuteronomy 12:32* .. 172
*Deuteronomy 18:20-22* ............................... 132
*Deuteronomy 30:9* .... 198
*Deuteronomy 31:6* ...... 50
*Deuteronomy 32:15-18* ............................... 196
*Deuteronomy 32:21* . 193, 195
*Deuteronomy 32:28-30* ....................... 109, 121
*Deuteronomy 7:2-6* ..... 51
*Deuteronomy 7:6* ........ 21
*Deuteronomy 9:11-12* . 29
*Deuteronomy 9:15-19* . 30

## E

*Ecclesiastes 1:2* .......... 195
*Ephesians 1:22* ............ 41
*Ephesians 2:8* ............ 221
*Ephesians 5:26* .......... 131
*Exodus 17:6-7* ........... 186
*Exodus 17:8-16* ......... 187
*Exodus 19:5-6* ............. 24
*Exodus 19:7-8* ............. 25
*Exodus 20:18-19* ......... 26
*Exodus 23:21* ............. 215
*Exodus 23:31-33* ... 51, 52
*Exodus 24:12* ............... 28
*Exodus 24:3* ................. 27
*Exodus 24:4-8* ............. 27
*Exodus 24:9-11* ........... 28
*Exodus 25:8-9* ............. 31
*Exodus 34:10* ............... 22
*Exodus 34:12* ....... 93, 101
*Ezekiel 23: 12-16* ....... 151
*Ezekiel 23:1-10* .......... 146
*Ezekiel 23:1-49* .......... 145
*Ezekiel 23:18* ............. 146
*Ezekiel 23:22-23* ........ 151
**Ezekiel 23:35**............. 147
*Ezekiel 23:48* ............. 148
*Ezekiel 23:49* ............. 148
*Ezekiel 23:5-7* ............ 151

## G

*Galatians 3:24* ............. 36
*Genesis 1:27* ................ 55

## H

*Hebrews 10:19* ............ 43
*Hebrews 10:19-22* ....... 44
**Hebrews 10:29**........... 53
*Hebrews 13:20-21* ....... 40

*Hebrews 13:8* ............ 205
*Hebrews 7:25-26* ......... 42
*Hebrews 8:1-5* ............. 33
*Hebrews 9:1-14* ........... 36
*Hebrews 9:24-26* ......... 38

## I

*Isaiah 29:13* ............... 143
*Isaiah 45:22* ............... 153
*Isaiah 5:20-21* ............ 149

## J

*James 4:4* ..................... 62
*Jeremiah 10:10* ............. 79
*Jeremiah 17:9* ............... 88
*Jeremiah 29:11* ........... 199
*Jeremiah 29:13* ............. 16
*Jeremiah 3:1* ................. 18
*Jeremiah 7:1-4* ........... 142
*Jeremiah 7:25-28* ....... 151
*Jeremiah 7:4* ............... 143
*Jeremiah 7:5-10* ......... 143
*Joel 2:32* .................... 214
*Joel 3:1-21* ................. 192
*John 1:49* ..................... 15
*John 10:10* ................. 203
*John 10:30* ................... 39
*John 10:7-14* .............. 122
*John 14:6* ............... 15, 38

*John 18:37* ................... 15
*John 18:38* ................... 11
*John 3:14-18* .............. 218
*John 3:16* .................... 164
*John 4:23-24* .............. 203
*John 6:35* ..................... 41
*John 8:12* ..................... 41
*Joshua 24:31* ............... 70
*Joshua 7:1* .................. 187
*Judges 2:14-15* ............. 71
*Judges 2:16-19* ............. 71
*Judges 2:19* .................. 72
*Judges 21:24-25* ........... 73

## L

*Leviticus 18:25-30* .... 140
*Leviticus 20:10* .......... 147

## M

*Mark 13:22-23* ............. 12
*Mark 13:33* ................... 66
*Mark 4:9* ...................... 78
*Matthew 24:24-25* ....... 66
*Matthew 24:4-5* ........... 65
*Matthew 24:4-51* ......... 66
*Matthew 25:31-46* ..... 192
*Matthew 7:13-16* .......... 50
*Micah 6:8* .......... 185, 192

## N

*Numbers 22:12............ 57*
*Numbers 23:17-24 ...... 58*
*Numbers 23:7-10 ........ 57*
*Numbers 25:1-2 .......... 60*
*Numbers 31:16............ 60*

## P

*Proverbs 28:13 .......... 150*
*Psalm 119:1-8 ............. 76*
*Psalm 139:224........... 104*
*Psalm 139:23-24 ......... 78*
*Psalm 145:17................ 76*
*Psalm 19:7-11 .............. 92*
*Psalm 25:1-4 .............. 183*
*Psalm 30:5...................... 6*
*Psalm 48:1-2 ............. 139*
*Psalm 61:1-4 ............. 202*
*Psalm 68:8-13 ........... 198*
*Psalm 95:10-11 ......... 187*
*Psalm 97:5-7 ............. 123*

## R

*Revelation 12:11 ....... 208*
*Revelation 2:14 ... 19, 200*
*Revelation 2:20 ........... 18*
*Revelation 2:20-21 .... 200*
*Romans 10:10: .......... 223*
*Romans 10:12-15 ..... 214, 216*
*Romans 3:20 ............... 36*
*Romans 8:3 ........... 32, 34*

## BOOKS BY JEANNE METCALF

**An Arsenal of Powerful Prayers** [165]
Scriptural Prayers to Move Mountains
**Arising Incense**
A Believer's Priesthood
**Above Artificial Intelligence**
Finding God in a World of A.I.

---

[165] This is a book of written prayers of assorted topics to help believers live a stronger, active faith. No workbook.

**An End Time Church in Transition**
  Preparing for the King's Return
**Bible Study Basics**
  A Closer Look at God's Word
**Candidate for A Miracle**
  Wisdom from the Miracles of Yeshua
**Deceived**
  How Errors in a Faith System Affect Both God & His People
**Foundations of Revival**
  Biblical Evidence for Revival
**His Reflection**
  What God longs to see in His People
**Heaven's Greater Government**
  Behind the Scenes of Earth's Events
**In The Name of Yehovah We Set Up Our Banners**
  Biblical use of Banners

**It's All About Heaven**
As Pictured in Scripture
**Kingdom Keys for Kingdom Kids**
Walking in Kingdom Power
**Molded for the Miraculous**
Why God made You
**Our Secure Faith Heritage**
Foundational Truths to an Unshakeable Walk with God
**Releasing the Impossible**
The Limitless Power of Intercession
*Volume 1: Intercessions from the Author's Life*
*Volume 2: Intercessions from Biblical Characters*
*Workbook: Both Volumes compiled in Workbook.*
**Salvation Depicted in a Meal** [166]
An Hebraic Christian Guide to Passover
**The Coming Deception**
How to Recognize the Man of Sin, the Son of Perdition
**The Jeremiah Generation**
God's Response to Injustice
**The Warrior Bride-**
God's Kingdom Advancing through Spiritual Warfare
**Thy Kingdom Come**
Entering God's Rest in Prayer

---

[166] Haggadah (Guide) for a Christian Passover. No Workbook.

**Watching, Waiting, Warning**
  Obeying Yeshua's Command to Watch & Pray
**When Nations Rumble**
  A Study of the Book of Amos
**Worship in Spirit and In Truth** [167]
  The Tabernacle of David - Past, Present & Future

---

[167] Good sister book to "In the Name of YeHoVaH We Set Up Our Banners".

## ABOUT JEANNE METCALF

Jeanne believes the Word of God opens a door to help every believer to know their God. That knowledge, once gleaned and retained, makes strong believers to help them stand in the real world in which we live, no matter their vocation.

With these convictions in mind, Jeanne, inspired and led by the Holy Spirit, began to write in the 1990's. Soon she developed inductive[168] style Bible Studies and self-published them for her students to use. With her major goal to equip the saints, she found that her sound teachings, presented with clarity and simplicity, made an impact. As long as her listeners put in their valuable time to study scripture and took Jeanne's advice to call upon the Holy Spirit to help them, they became powerful believers, transformed, prepared and ready to stand in their generation.

Today, past students who studied the Bible with Jeanne, as well current new students, testify as to the validity of Jeanne's writing and teaching gift. They

---

[168] In the inductive Bible Study method, believers learn first by reading and studying the Word on their own, then they glean from the textbook. This study method often gives a better foundation to a believer's faith than sitting through lectures or speaker related teachings.

love the clarity and simplicity of the Word as she presents it in a refreshing straightforward format. Thus, they encouraged Jeanne to make her books more widely available.

Therefore, Jeanne began Cegullah Publishing, and then a year later, opened Cegullah Apologetic Academy. The academy, in addition to presenting accredited, Bible Study material, invites all believers to read or study the Word of God, and thereby, be strong in YeHoVaH and the strength of His might.

A greater availability of Jeanne's works *(as well as other authors which Cegullah Publishing looks forward to publishing in the future)*, opens doors for more people to know their God and do exploits!

**"But the people that know their God shall be strong and do exploits".** *Daniel 11:32 b*

\*\*\*\*\*\*\*\*\*\*\*\*\*\*\*\*\*\*\*\*\*\*\*\*\*\*\*\*\*\*\*\*\*\*\*\*\*\*\*\*\*\*\*\*\*\*\*\*\*\*\*\*\*\*\*\*\*\*\*

*P.S. Recent inquiries require acknowledging the correct way to address Jeanne. While she is comfortable with people addressing her on a first name basis, her official title is Rev. Dr. Jeanne Metcalf.*

\*\*\*\*\*\*\*\*\*\*\*\*\*\*\*\*\*\*\*\*\*\*\*\*\*\*\*\*\*\*\*\*\*\*\*\*\*\*\*\*\*\*\*\*\*\*\*\*\*\*\*\*\*\*\*\*\*\*\*

# ABOUT CP & AA

## CEGULLAH PUBLISHING & APOLOGETICS ACADEMY.

We publish books and operate an accredited academy:

- **OUR PUBLISHING ARM** provides opportunities for our reading audience to explore pertinent topics which steady, reaffirm, and help them to walk out their life in victory.

  **Our Publishing Motto:**
  *Publishing the treasures of modern-day scribes.*

- **OUR ACADEMY** presents accredited courses for those students who wish to study to obtain their degree, either bachelor, master or doctorate.

  **Our Academy Motto:**
  *Earnestly contend for the faith once given to the saints.*

**Our Overall Vision**
- To supply Christian, Bible-based materials for readers and students study God's Word

**Our Overall Focus**
- To help our readers and students to know **what they believe and why.**

**Our Overall Mission**
- To provide Bible educational tools to assist readers or accredited students to know their God and connect with Him.

## CONTACT INFORMATION
www.cegullahpublishing.ca

| i-Stock Pictures used in this book. | |
| --- | --- |
| Cover Picture | 657028012 |
| Open Bible | 507001752 |
| Lady with silencing finger | 1334677935 |
| Fake/Fact Picture | 1555376746 |
| Ketubah Writing | 1090742314 |